GCSE Projects in Access 2000

P. Evans B.Sc. (Hons)

Published by
Payne-Gallway Publishers Ltd
an imprint of Harcourt Education Ltd
Halley Court, Jordan Hill
Oxford OX2 8EJ

E-mail info@payne-gallway.co.uk

2002

A catalogue entry for this book is available from the British Library.

10-digit ISBN: 1 903112 54 0
13-digit ISBN: 978 1 903112 54 0

Copyright © Phill Evans 2002

First edition 2002

10 09 08 07 06
10 9 8 7 6 5 4 3 2

Printed in Great Britain by
WM Print Ltd
Walsall
West Midlands

Acknowledgements

I would like to thank Pat Heathcote and everyone at Payne-Gallway Publishers for their patience, support and advice in preparing this text. I am grateful to colleagues and students at Clough Hall Technology School for their assistance, in particular Alan Nussey, Anthony Holley, Mark Cartledge, Peter Leese, Neil Venables, Alison Shaw and Adele Shaw. Special thanks go to Nick Wheat for his invaluable help and support. Finally, I would like to dedicate this book to the memory of Kathleen Marshall.

Preface

This book is designed to help students on a GCSE ICT full course such as AQA (Specification A) or OCR (ICT A) complete a major project using MS Access 2000.

Step-by-step instructions are given on how to choose, design, implement and document a database system at GCSE level. Detailed examples from a sample project are included throughout the text. Structured tasks and related resources are provided for students. These provide a detailed framework around which a successful database project can be developed. All of the resources referred to within the text can be freely downloaded from www.payne-gallway.co.uk.

It is important to note that every Examination Board places emphasis on different aspects of project work, and to get the best possible results close attention should always be paid to the current project marking criteria and official exemplar materials. The project marking criteria for AQA (Specification A) are included in the Appendix. Further information and guidance for this specification can also be found at: www.aqa.org.uk/qual/gcse/ict_a.html.

Contents

Part 1 – Analysis

Part 2 – Design

Part 3 – Implementation

Appendix

Index

Part 1 – Analysis

This section covers the following topics:

Introduction

During the analysis stage of your project you must investigate the existing system to identify exactly what the problems are with it. During this investigation you should use a variety of fact-finding methods to gather information. These include interviewing people, watching them at work, designing and handing out questionnaires and looking at paperwork. Once you have completed your investigation you must produce a detailed description of how the existing system works and consider alternative ways of solving the problems. You must describe your chosen solution and produce a set of system objectives – this is a list of the tasks that the new system must be able to carry out. A set of performance criteria should also be produced which describes how the new system should perform in order to meet the system objectives.

Chapter 1

The system life cycle

The **system life cycle** is the series of stages that are worked through during the development of a new information system. The stages of the system life cycle are shown in Figure 1.1 below. In order to produce a good GCSE project you must work through the stages of the system life cycle to produce an ICT-based system that solves the information-handling problems of a real business, organisation or individual. It is important that you understand the different types of activities that take place during each stage of the system life cycle – this chapter describes what these are.

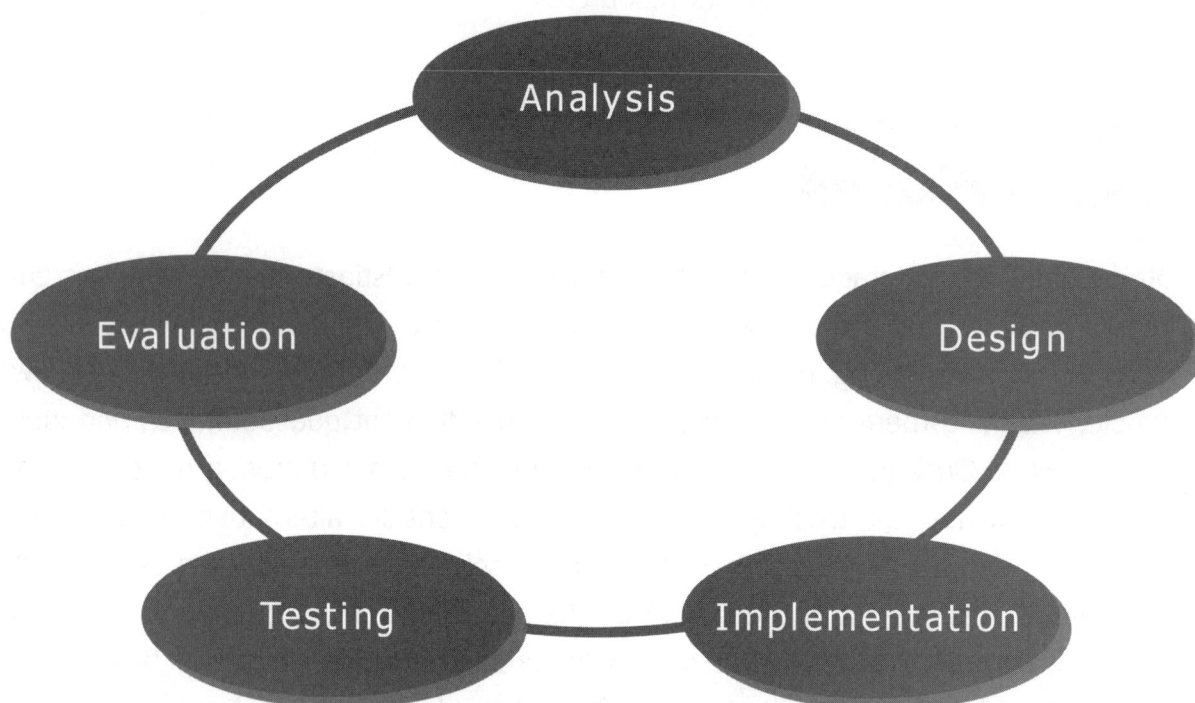

Figure 1.1: The stages of the system life cycle

Analysis

During the analysis stage **systems analysts** investigate the existing system to identify exactly what the problems are with it. During their investigation the systems analysts use a variety of **fact-finding methods** to gather information. These include interviewing people, watching them at work, designing and handing out questionnaires and looking at paperwork.

Once the systems analysts have completed their investigation they produce a detailed description of how the existing system works. This contains information about the data that is stored, where it is stored, how it flows around the system and how it is processed. This information is often represented using diagrams as well as words – **data flow diagrams** are often used to do this.

Different ways of solving the problems are then considered. The best and most cost-effective way is identified and adopted as the **chosen solution**. A set of **system objectives** is then produced. This is a list of the tasks that the new system must be able to carry out. A set of **performance criteria** is produced along with the system objectives. These describe how the new system should perform in order to meet the system objectives.

Design

During the design stage a **system design specification** is produced. This describes the new system in detail and contains information about the following:

- **Input**
  - What data will need to be input?
  - Where does the input data come from?
  - How will data be input?
  - What will any input screens need to look like and have on them?

- **Output**
  - What output is required from the system?
  - What output methods will be used?
  - What layout is needed on printed output?
  - What will output screens need to look like and have on them?

- **Data storage**
  - What data files are needed?
  - What fields will the records in each file need?
  - How will data be checked to make sure that it is sensible and correct?

- **User interface**
  - Which type of user interface will be used?
  - What options will be available to users?

- **Backup and recovery procedures**
  - What methods will be used to back up the system?
  - How often will backups be carried out?
  - Where will backup copies be kept?
  - How will data be restored if it is lost or damaged?

- **Security procedures**
  - How will data be protected from unauthorised access?
  - Will some users need different levels of access from other users?

- **Test plan**

  A plan of the testing that will be carried out on the new system is prepared. This should include details of the purpose of each test, the test data that will be used and what the expected result is.

Implementation

The implementation stage involves setting up the system described in the design specification. Activities at this stage include:

- creating data files
- entering enough data so that the system can be tested
- creating input and output screens
- setting up the user interface
- setting up system security

Testing

During the testing stage the tests specified in the test plan are carried out to make sure that all the parts of the system work correctly. Three categories of **test data** are used during testing – **normal**, **extreme** and **erroneous**. These are used to make sure that the system will work under normal, boundary or borderline conditions and that data containing errors will be rejected.

If any faults are found the system is modified to try and correct them. The modified parts of the system are then tested again to make sure that the faults have been corrected.

Once the system is working correctly, **documentation** is prepared for it: there are two types of documentation – **technical documentation** and **user documentation**.

- Technical documentation describes a system in detail in terms that a systems analyst or programmer can understand if changes need to be made to it. This will include things like:

  - the system design specification
  - data flow diagrams
  - a description of the various parts of the system and what each one does
  - input and output screen layouts
  - the user interface design
  - the test plan

- User documentation provides the people who will be using a system with information about what it can do, how to operate it and how to deal with error messages. Good user documentation should contain the following sections:

  - a description of what the system is designed to do
  - the minimum hardware and software requirements of the system
  - instructions on how to load and run the system
  - detailed instructions on how to operate each part of the system
  - error messages, their meaning and how to deal with them
  - where to get more help, such as telephone support lines and on-line tutorials

Evaluation

During this stage of the life cycle the effectiveness of the final solution is considered by looking back at the system objectives and performance criteria to see if they have been met. The various parts of the new system that satisfy different system objectives are identified. How well these parts measured up to the performance criteria during the system testing is discussed. Any limitations of the system are identified – these could be either objectives that haven't been met or that were only partially met. The reasons for these limitations are explained and might refer to technical problems or time constraints. Finally the ways that the new system could be improved in the future are discussed. These could include ways that any limitations may be overcome or even completely new features that it would be useful to add at some point.

Exercise 1

1. The system life cycle describes the stages that are worked through when a new computer system is being developed.

    (a) List the stages of the system life cycle given below in the correct order.
       The first one has been done for you.

       Design
       Implementation
       Analysis
       Feasibility study
       Evaluation
       Testing

       Stage 1   Feasibility study
       Stage 2
       Stage 3
       Stage 4
       Stage 5
       Stage 6   (5)

    (b) Give **two** activities that would take place during the analysis stage of the system life cycle.   (2)

(c) Give **two** activities that would take place during the design stage of the system life cycle. (2)

(d) Give **three** different types of test data that should be used during the testing stage of the system life cycle. (3)

(e) Give **three** topics that should be included in the user documentation for a new computer system. (3)

(f) Give **three** topics that should be included in the technical documentation for a new computer system. (3)

AQA (NEAB) 2001 Paper 2 Tier F

2. When a new computerised system is being developed it is important that it is properly tested and documented.

(a) A package processes examination marks. When the marks are input they have to be validated with a range check. Marks are allowed if they are in the range 0 to 100.

Give **three** numbers you would use to test the range check worked correctly. Explain why you would carry out each of your three tests. (6)

(b) Documentation supplied with a system should provide instructions for normal use. Describe **three** other topics which should be included in the User Guide. (3)

AQA (NEAB) 1998 Paper 2 Tier F

3. The partners of a doctors' surgery are considering using a computer system to store patient records and handle appointments. A systems analyst is called in to carry out a feasibility study.

(a) Explain why a feasibility study is carried out. (3)

(b) After the feasibility study, the decision is made to go ahead with the introduction of the computer system. The systems analyst then carries out a detailed analysis of the existing system. Give **three** ways that the systems analyst could find out about the existing system. (3)

(c) After the analysis the systems analyst then produces a design specification for the new system. Give **four** items that should be included in the design specification. (4)

AQA (NEAB) 2000 Paper 2 Tier F

Chapter 2

Choosing a project

This book describes how to produce a major project for GCSE using a database package. This means that the problem you choose must be one that is best solved by setting up a database. You will need to look for problems where information in the form of paper-based records is being stored, searched through and sorted by hand.

Finding a user

To get the best possible marks you must try to come up with a situation that is real – don't just make something up! Your teacher will be able to give you some ideas and there are also some described in this chapter. These ideas are really just here to point you in the right direction. Once you've decided what sort of problem you'd like to tackle you should try to find a real person with a similar type of problem.

A good starting point is often parents or other teachers at school. Explain to them what a database is and ask if they have any problems handling information that might be solved by setting one up. Another possibility is employers – if you have a part-time job there may be a problem where you work that needs solving. You could also try finding out how information is handled at your local newsagent, estate agent, hotel, garage, travel agent, library, corner shop, restaurant, video store, cinema, theatre, sports centre, youth club, doctor's or dentist's surgery.

Wherever you look it is important that you find out exactly what is being done with the information that is being stored. The worst kinds of projects are those that just store a lot of information in a database and nothing more ever happens to it. If this is the case you might as well just put all the information in a box and lock it in a cupboard – it would be quicker than going to the time and trouble of setting up a database! To avoid falling into this trap look for the input, processing and output that is going on in the existing system – do this by asking yourself the following questions.

Input

- What data is being input to the system?
- Where does this data come from?
- How often is this data input?

Processing

- What happens to data after it has been input?
- Is the data changed, used to generate other data, searched through or sorted?

Output

- What happens to data after it has been processed?
- Is it displayed on the screen or printed out in the form of a list or report?

Finally ask yourself the question, "Does this all happen more than once?" You won't get good marks for a 'one-off' system that will only ever be used once. A good GCSE project is one that produces a **reusable system** for a **real user**.

Project ideas

These ideas are here to help you understand the sort of topics that are suitable for a project. You should use them as a starting point for deciding on a project of your own.

Project	Input	Processing	Output
Corner Shop	Stock details (description, price, current stock level, reorder level)	Add, edit and delete stock details.	Product details on screen.
	Supplier details (name, address)	Add, edit and delete supplier details.	Supplier details on screen.
		Look up supplier details.	Lists of products that need re-ordering.
		Look up stock details.	Printed orders to send to suppliers.
		Search for stock that needs reordering.	Sales analysis reports.

Project	Input	Processing	Output
Dating Agency	Client details (name, address, telephone number, hobbies, interests)	Look up client details. Add, edit and delete client details. Search for people matching individual client's requirements.	Client details on screen. Lists of compatible clients on screen. Printed reports for clients listing details of people matching their requirements.
Estate Agent	House details (address, selling price etc.) Client details (name, address etc.)	Look up client details. Look up house details. Add, edit and delete client details. Add, edit and delete house details. Search for houses matching client's requirements.	House details on screen. Client details on screen. Printed lists of compatible houses. Letters to clients with details of compatible houses.
Garage	Customer details (name, address, car registration) Car details (registration number, make, model) Job details (customer, date booked in, return date, fault, parts needed, cost)	Look up customer details. Add, edit and delete customer details. Look up job details. Add, edit and delete job details. Look up car details. Add, edit and delete car details. Search for available dates and times for jobs to be carried out. Search for jobs booked in for a particular day.	Customer details on screen. Car details on screen. Job details on screen. Printed lists of jobs for a day, customer details and parts needed. Print invoices for customers.

Project	Input	Processing	Output
Hotel	Guest details (name and address) Booking details (date, time, type of room booked, length of stay) Room details (room number, number of beds, bathroom, other facilities, price per night)	Look up guest details. Add, edit and delete guest details. Look up room details. Add, edit and delete room details. Look up booking details. Add, edit and delete booking details. Search for available rooms for particular dates.	Guest details on screen. Room booking details on screen. Printed report listing guests arriving and rooms that need preparing for a certain date. Printed bills for guests leaving on a certain date.
Library	Member details (name, address, date of birth, telephone number) Book details (ISBN, title, author, subject) Loan details (book, member, date due back)	Look up member details. Look up book details. Look up loan details. Search for books matching member's requirements. Search for overdue books.	Member details on screen. Book details on screen. Loan details on screen. Lists of books matching member's requirements on screen or as a printed report. Printed report listing overdue books. Letters to members with overdue books. Printed membership cards.

Project	Input	Processing	Output
Newsagent	Customer details (name and address) Newspaper details (name and price) Delivery details (round, customer, newspaper, day)	Look up customer details. Add, edit and delete delivery details. Add, edit and delete customer details. Look up delivery details. Search for deliveries for a round on a particular date.	Delivery details on screen. Lists of daily deliveries for each round. Bills for customers.
Restaurant	Customer details (name and address) Booking details (date, time, number in party, table number) Table details (table number, maximum number of people)	Look up customer details. Add, edit and delete booking details. Add, edit and delete customer details. Look up booking details. Search for available tables on a particular date at a particular time. Search for bookings on a particular date.	Booking details on screen. Lists of daily bookings. Letters to customers advertising special promotions and events.

Project	Input	Processing	Output
Sports Centre	Member details (name and address) Booking details (date, time, facility booked, charge)	Look up member details. Add, edit and delete booking details. Add, edit and delete member details. Look up booking details. Search for availability of facilities on a certain date. Search for bookings for a particular date.	Booking details on screen. Member details on screen. Printed membership cards. Printed lists of daily bookings and charges due to be paid. Letters to members advertising special promotions and events.
Theatre	Customer details (name and address) Performance details (date, time, number of seats available) Booking details (customer, date, time, performance, number of seats booked)	Look up customer details. Add, edit and delete seat booking details. Add, edit and delete customer details. Look up seat booking details. Search for available seats for a particular performance on a certain date.	Customer details on screen. Booking details on screen. Printed report of seat sales analysis for a performance. Letters to customers advertising future performances. Printed tickets.

Project proposal

Once you've decided on a project, the next step is to write a brief summary of what you're going to do. This will need to be shown to your teacher who will check it for you. In this book we're going to work through solving the information-handling problems of a small video rental shop called **MovieZone**. The proposal for this project is shown below.

Project title   MovieZone Video Rental System

Aims of project

To investigate and try to solve the information-handling problems of MovieZone, a small video rental shop in Stoke-on-Trent. The owners of the shop want me to design and set up a more efficient way of storing and handling information about videos, members and loans.

Input	Processing	Output
Member details (member number, name, address, date of birth)	Look up member details	Member details
	Look up video details	Video details
Video details (video number, title, category, certificate)	Look up loan details	Loan details
	Search for videos matching member's requirements	Reports listing videos matching member's requirements
Loan details (video number, member number, length of loan, date due back)	Search for overdue videos	List of overdue videos
		Letters to members who have overdue videos

Task 2.1

Writing a project proposal

After completing this task you should have written a proposal for your own project like the one shown on the last page. To do this follow the steps listed below.

- Open the Word file **ProjectProposal.doc** (your teacher will provide this for you or it can be downloaded from the Student section at www.payne-gallway.co.uk). You will see the template shown below.

- First enter a title for your project in this box.

Project title	

Aims of project

Input	Processing	Output

- Next enter the aims of the project in this box.
  Start by identifying who your project is for – this will normally be the name of a business or individual. Then go on to describe what you're planning to do for them. You don't need to write a lot here, just enough to give the person reading it an idea of what you want to do.

- Finally complete the **input**, **processing** and **output** columns. These are to show what data goes into the system, what happens to it and what comes out of the system. Remember if nothing's happening to the data, it's not worth doing!

- Save and print your work. Give the printout to your teacher so that they can read it and give you some advice and feedback before you go any further.

Chapter 3

Finding out about the current system

During this stage of your project work you are taking on the role of a systems analyst by trying to identify and investigate the problems with the existing system. You will do this by getting answers to questions such as "what is being done now?", "why is it being done?", "who is doing it?" and "how is it being done?". There are many different ways of gathering information about a system such as using questionnaires, interviewing people and examining paperwork. You don't have to do all of these things but it will help you to produce a better analysis if you do at least some of them.

Questionnaires

Questionnaires are a useful way of gathering a lot of information quickly. People are often more honest and say what they really think about a system if they are filling in an anonymous questionnaire rather than being asked face-to-face in an interview. It is also much easier to analyse the responses given on a well-designed questionnaire than notes taken during interviews.

Designing a questionnaire

- Start with a title and introduction explaining the purpose of the questionnaire and encouraging people to complete it.
- Keep it short and simple. Try to keep to one or two sheets of A4 with questions that don't involve too much writing.
- Think carefully about why you need each question. If you don't know what will you do with the information from a question don't use it.
- Try to make the first few questions easy and pleasant to answer. This will encourage people to fill in the questionnaire. Difficult questions at the beginning of a questionnaire can be very off-putting – leave these until the end.

There are three main types of question that can be used in a questionnaire:

1. Multiple-choice questions that offer a limited number of choices.

E.g. What is your favourite day of the week?

☐ Monday
☐ Tuesday
☐ Wednesday
☐ Thursday
☐ Friday
☐ Saturday
☐ Sunday
☐ No preference

2. Questions that ask for a value or number.

E.g. Please give your age   _____

3. Questions that ask for an opinion or suggestion.

E.g. How can we improve our service?

_____

_____

The questionnaire shown over the page was designed and used to collect information from the customers of the MovieZone video shop.

MovieZone Customer Questionnaire

This questionnaire will help us find out what you think about the service currently offered by MovieZone and try to improve it. Your opinions are very important to us. As a thank you for completing this form we will give you one night's free rental of any new release.

1. What is your favourite type of movie?

    ☐ Action
    ☐ Comedy
    ☐ Horror
    ☐ Science fiction
    ☐ Thriller
    ☐ Romance
    ☐ Other   please state _____

2. How many times a week do you rent a movie?

    ☐ Once
    ☐ Twice
    ☐ Three times
    ☐ More   please state _____

3. How easy is it to find out if we have a particular movie available for rental?

    ☐ Generally quite easy
    ☐ Generally quite difficult
    ☐ Don't know

4. Approximately how many minutes does it usually take you from choosing a movie to leaving the shop with it?

    _____ minutes

5. How can we improve our service?

_____

_____

_____

_____

_____

6. Please write your name and membership number in the spaces provided below.

First name ☐ ☐ ☐ ☐ ☐ ☐ ☐ ☐ ☐ ☐ ☐ ☐ ☐

Surname ☐ ☐ ☐ ☐ ☐ ☐ ☐ ☐ ☐ ☐ ☐ ☐

Membership number ☐ ☐ ☐ ☐

That's the end of the questionnaire!

Thank you for taking the time to complete it.

Please hand it in to receive your free movie rental

voucher (one per customer only).

Task 3.1

Designing a questionnaire for your project

After completing this task you should have designed a questionnaire for your own project similar to the example shown on the last two pages. The questionnaire should aim to gather information that tells you what people who use the existing system think about it. Follow the steps below to do this.

- Start with a blank sheet of paper – you'll need to write some ideas down and produce an initial design away from the computer first.
- On your paper:
  — Write a title for the questionnaire.
  — Write a short introduction explaining the purpose of the questionnaire and encouraging people to complete it.
  — Write down the questions that you want to ask. Think carefully about why each question is needed – what will it help you find out? If you don't know what you will do with the information from a question don't use it.
  — Decide how each question will be answered. Will a set of multiple-choice answers, a space for a value to be entered or lines for an opinion to be written down be best?
  — Check that you have made the first few questions easy to answer and that any difficult questions have been left until the end.
- Load a word processing package and create a new blank document. Work from your paper design to produce a word-processed version of the questionnaire.
- When your questionnaire is finished print out one copy and get a friend to complete it. Ask them how easy it was to fill in and if they have any ideas about how it could be improved.
- Make any final improvements to the questionnaire before printing enough copies to give out to the people who must complete it. Remember there's no need to give out hundreds of questionnaires! A small sensible number (e.g. 20) is enough to get some idea about what people think. You'll need to keep at least one completed copy of the questionnaire to include as evidence in your final project report.
- Include in your final report a short analysis of what your questionnaires told you. This just needs to be a summary of the main points, illustrated with a few graphs.

Interviews

Interviewing the people who use a system is often a good way of gathering detailed information about it. This can be time-consuming if a lot of people need interviewing. The set of questions used for the MovieZone project are shown below along with the answers given by Mr and Mrs Marshall, the owners of the shop.

MovieZone Interview Questions and Answers

1. What information do you store?

We store information about members, videos and videos that are on loan.

2. How and where do you store information?

Information about members is stored on cards which are kept in a card index box. Each member has his or her own card. Information about each video is stored on a card, which is kept inside its case. Information about videos on loan is written down in a list.

3. What happens when you get new videos?

A new video details card is written out and put inside its case. The information on these cards is changed if the video details change or it is thrown away or sold.

4. What happens when new members join?

Cards are added when a new member joins. We give the new member two blank member details cards to complete. We keep one and the other becomes their membership card. The information on the cards is changed when a member changes their details such as their address. Member cards are destroyed when a member leaves.

5. What happens when someone rents a video?

The video cases are stored on the shelves at the back of the shop. There are no videos in the cases – we keep these behind the counter arranged in order of video number. Customers look through the shelves to find the videos they want to rent and take the cases to the counter. When a video is rented the member's details are taken from their membership card and video details are taken from the card inside its case. This information is written down in the loans list. The videocassette is taken from behind the counter and put in the video case which is then handed to the customer.

6. How much does it cost to rent a video?

We charge £2.00 per day for every film. Members can rent videos for up to 3 days.

7. What happens when someone returns a video?

*When a video is returned the details in the loan list are **X**ed out.*

8. How do you deal with overdue videos?

We look through the loans list at the end of every day to see if any videos are overdue and write out a list of members with overdue videos. This list is used to prepare reminder letters, which are posted to the members with overdue videos.

9. What problems does the current system cause?

Members often forget to bring their membership cards and sometimes even lose them. If this happens their details have to be looked up by searching through the members card index box for their card. This can be very time-consuming and often causes long queues in the shop;

The video details cards often go missing from the cases and new ones have to be written out by hand.

Member details cards are often put in the wrong place in the members box and it takes time to find them when a member's details need to be looked up.

We can't tell if videos are available without looking through the loans list and searching through the video cases on the shelves.

Different members of staff complete the loans list and it is often difficult to read other people's handwriting, which can sometimes lead to mistakes.

It takes a long time to look through the loans list and write out a list of overdue videos.

It takes a long time to write out reminder letters to members with overdue videos because the details for each member have to be looked up in the members card index box and transferred by hand to a letter along with the video details.

10. What experience of using computers do you have?

We do have a computer but it doesn't get used too much because none of us are really confident using it.

11. What computer hardware and software do you have now?

We bought our computer about three years ago. You're welcome to have a look and see if it will be any use.

12. Do you have any money to spend on developing a new system?

We can spend up to £1000 if necessary.

Task 3.2

Preparing some interview questions

After completing this task you should have written a set of interview questions for your own project similar to those in the example shown on the last two pages. The interview questions should aim to find out more about how the current system works and what the problems are with it. Follow the steps below to do this.

- Start with a blank sheet of paper – you'll need to write some ideas down about the questions that you're going to ask.
- On your paper write down the questions that you want to ask. Think carefully about why each question is needed – what will it help you find out? If you don't know what you will do with the information from a question don't use it.
- Load a word processing package and create a new document. Work from your paper design to produce a word-processed version of the interview questions. Remember to include enough space to write down the answers when you actually carry out the interview.
- Carry out the interview with your user. Ask them each question and write down their answers. If you need to ask them other questions as a result of what they tell you write these down along with the answers on a separate sheet of paper.
- Keep your completed set of interview notes safe. You will need to refer to them again and include them in your project report. You may want to actually produce a word-processed version of the questions and answers. This isn't absolutely necessary provided of course that your handwriting can be read!

Observation

Watching people use a system can often give a more accurate picture than interviews or questionnaires of what actually happens. The problems with this method are that people can find it threatening to be watched while they are working and quite a lot of time is consumed as little useful information is gathered during short observations. If you decide to do any observation you will need to write some short notes about what you saw.

Examining documents

Looking at the paperwork that is used in the existing system is an important way of understanding how it works. This is what the term 'examining documents' actually means. You must look for and collect examples of how information is gathered or stored. These could be forms that are completed, index cards or paper records from manual filing systems, letters, memos or reports.

For the MovieZone system we will need examples of documents to show how information about members, videos and loans is stored and handled. The results of the interview told us that information about members and videos is stored on cards. We also found out that loan information is written down on a daily loans list and overdue letters are produced using a blank standard letter. Examples of these documents are shown in Figures 3.1 to 3.4. You should include examples like these in your own project report.

Member Number: 101

Name: Heather Porter

Address: 12 Hilltop Road

Talke, Stoke-on-Trent,

Staffordshire, ST8 8NQ

Date of birth 28-11-87

Figure 3.1: A MovieZone member details card

Video Number: __112__

Title: __Crouching Tiger, Hidden Dragon__

Category: __Action__

Certificate: __12__

Figure 3.2: A MovieZone video details card

Date: __22/4/01__

Member Number	Video Number	Length of Loan	Date Due
107	119	2	24/4/01
98	57	3	24/4/01
117	117	2	23/4/01
124	157	1	23/4/01
118	102	2	24/4/01
109	126	3	25/4/01
114	166	2	24/4/01
136	101	1	23/4/01
156	201	1	23/4/01

Figure 3.3: Part of a MovieZone loans list

Simon Shelley

9 Leighton Road

Talke

S-o-T, Staffordshire

ST8 9TC

Dear Mr Shelley

The videos listed below are now overdue and should be returned immediately. Failure to do so will result in a charge of £3.00 per day.

Video Number	Length of Loan	Date Due
103	2	5/10/01
118	1	4/10/01

Yours truly,

A and K Marshall
MOVIEZONE VIDEO RENTAL

8/10/01

Figure 3.4: A MovieZone overdue letter

Task 3.3

Collect some sample documents

After completing this task you should have collected examples of paperwork used in the existing system. You only need to include one example of any document and you should only include documents that show something relevant to what you're doing. For example if you're going to produce a system to handle seat bookings in a theatre <u>don't</u> include an example of an application form for a job in the theatre's bar! <u>Do</u> include something like a booking sheet showing seats available for a particular performance.

- Collect examples of documents that show how:
  - information is **gathered**, such as letters, memos or pre-printed forms
  - information is **stored**, such as index cards or paper records from manual filing systems
  - information is **output**, such as hand-written lists or reports

- You will need <u>one</u> copy of each document – this can be either a real copy or a photocopy. You must explain what each document shows and why it has been included.

Chapter 4

Describing the current system

After examining the current system you must use the information you have collected to produce a detailed description about how it works and the problems that need solving. This **problem description** should include information about:

- who the **real** end-user is – this will normally be the name of a business, organisation or individual
- the type of work that is carried out or the services that are provided by the real end-user
- the type of information that is collected and stored in order to do this work;
- how and where this information is stored
- the tasks that are carried out using this information
- the problems that are caused by the current system

The problem description for the MovieZone project is shown below. The information contained in it was collected through the use of questionnaires and an interview with Mr and Mrs Marshall, the owners of the shop. Other information was gathered by watching people at work in the shop.

Problem Description

This project will aim to solve the information-handling problems of MovieZone Video, a video rental service based in Kidsgrove, Stoke-on-Trent.

MovieZone rents videos out to customers who have completed an application form and become members. MovieZone currently has 90 members and a collection of 200 videos.

To do this work and provide these services, information is collected and stored about videos and members. Information about each video is written down on a card that is kept inside its case. Information about each member is written down on a card. These cards are stored in a card index box in ascending order of member number. Information about videos on loan is written down in a loans list each day.

When a customer wants to rent a video they take the empty case from the shelf and hand it in at the counter. The shop assistant takes the video number from the details card inside its case and asks the customer for their membership number. If the member doesn't know their membership number the assistant looks it up in the members card index box. The membership number and video number are written down on the loans list for that day. The shop assistant asks how many days the customer wants to rent the video for and writes this on the loans list for the day along with the date that the video will be due back. The shop assistant puts the videocassette inside the case and hands it to the customer. When a video is returned the assistant searches through the loans list for the day it was rented out and crosses out the entry. The videocassette is put away behind the counter and the empty case is placed back on the shelf.

At the end of every day the loans lists are searched to see if any videos haven't been returned. Overdue reminder letters are completed by hand and posted to any members who have overdue videos.

When a new member joins they are asked to fill in two member details cards. The shop assistant writes the membership number on both cards. One card is given back to the member – this is their membership card. The other card is put in the member details card index box.

When a new video is bought, a video details card is completed and put inside the case. The videocassette is put behind the counter and the empty case is placed on the shelves.

When a member leaves they are asked to hand in their membership card and it is destroyed along with their card from the member details box.

When a video is sold or thrown away because it is no longer popular or has worn out, the video details card is taken out of the case and destroyed.

The current system causes the following problems:

- Members sometimes lose their membership cards or forget to bring them. When this happens their details have to be looked up by searching through the members card index box for the card with their details on it. This can be very time-consuming and often causes long queues in the shop;
- The video details cards often go missing from the cases and new ones have to be written out;

- Different members of staff complete the video details cards and loans lists. It is difficult to read other people's handwriting, which often leads to mistakes;
- Member details cards are sometimes put in the wrong place in the members card index box and it takes time to find them when the member's details need to be looked up;
- If a particular video is not in the right place on the shelves it is difficult to tell if it is out on loan without searching the shelves and looking through the loans lists;
- Staff find it hard to keep up-to-date their knowledge of all the different videos that are available for rental. This makes it difficult to answer customers when they enquire about certain titles or types of video;
- It takes a long time to look through the loans lists to find out which videos are overdue and write out reminder letters.

Task 4.1

Writing a Problem Description

After completing this task you should have written a problem description for your own project. To do this follow the steps listed below.

- Open the Word file **ProblemDescription.doc** (your teacher will provide this for you or it can be downloaded from the Student section at www.payne-gallway.co.uk.) You will see the template shown below.

Problem Description

This project will aim to solve the information-handling problems of [put the name of the business, organisation or individual here].

[Describe the type of work that is carried out and the services that are provided here].

To do this work and provide these services information is collected and stored about [list the information that is collected and stored here]. [Describe exactly how and where this information is stored here].

[Describe the tasks that are carried out by people using the current system here].

The current system causes the following problems:

- [List the problems caused by the current system here].

In the spaces provided on this template enter the information listed below. You can use the example given for the MovieZone project on pages 28-30 to help.

- The name of the business, organisation or individual that you are carrying out the project for.

- Describe the type of work that is carried out and the services that are provided.

- Describe the information that is collected and stored in order to do this work.

- Describe the different tasks that are carried out by people who use the current system. This is where you must describe in detail <u>what</u> is being done and <u>how</u> it is being done.

- List the problems caused by the current system.

- Save your work using a sensible filename.

Chapter 5

Drawing data flow diagrams

A data flow diagram describes how data flows through a system. Data flow diagrams are concerned only with data and do not describe hardware. Drawing data flow diagrams will help you to describe how the current system works. You might need some help from a teacher if you haven't done this before but it is an important part of the analysis stage of the system life cycle. The symbols used in data flow diagrams are described below in Figure 5.1.

External entity – this can represent either a source of input or destination for the output from a process.

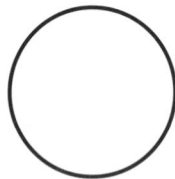

Process – this is something that happens to data. This box should be labelled with the name of the process that is taking place.

Data store – this is a place where data is stored such as a file held on disk, a batch of documents, papers in a filing cabinet, cards in a card index box, mail in an in-tray.

Data flow – these arrows represent pipelines through which data moves and show how it flows between entities, processes or data stores. The arrow should be labelled to describe what data is involved.

Figure 5.1: The symbols used in data flow diagrams

The data flow diagrams for the MovieZone system are shown below.

Updating member information

Member information is stored on individual cards in the members card index box. This information needs to be updated when a new member joins, when an existing member changes their details or when a member leaves.

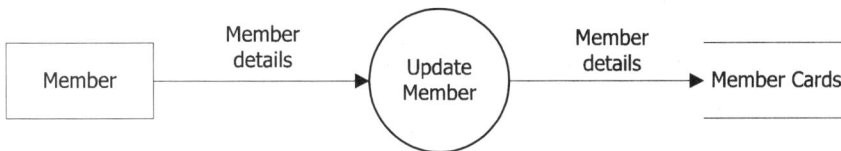

This data flow diagram shows that member details come from a member and move through the update process before being stored in the members card index.

Updating video information

Video information is stored on individual cards in the video cases. This information needs to be updated when a new video is purchased, when an existing video's details change or when a video is thrown away or sold.

This data flow diagram shows that video details come from a video and move through the update process before being stored on a video details card.

Dealing with customer enquiries

The video information on the video details cards is searched when a member asks if certain types of video or specific videos are available.

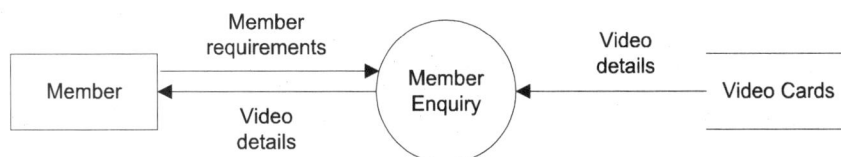

This data flow diagram shows that member enquires are dealt with by searching the video details cards to find videos matching a member's requirements. The details of any videos found are given to the member.

Loaning and returning videos

Information is added to the loans book when a member rents a video and removed when a video is returned.

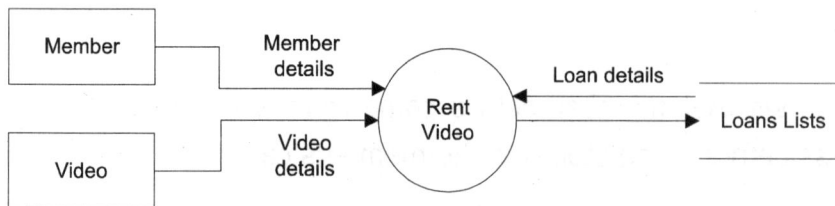

This data flow diagram shows that when a video is rented, member details are taken from the member and video details are taken from the video. These details are recorded in the loans list. When a video is returned, loan details are crossed out on the loans list.

Overdue videos

The information in the loans lists is searched at the end of every day to find out if any videos are overdue.

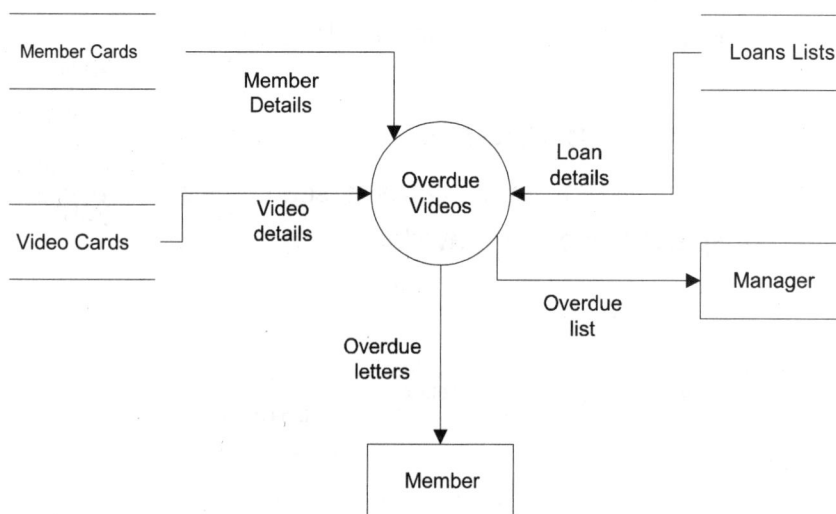

This data flow diagram shows that the information in the loans book is searched to find overdue videos. This information is used to produce a list of overdue videos for the shop's manager. It is also combined with information from the member and video card index boxes to produce reminder letters to members with overdue videos.

These data flow diagrams could be combined to form a single diagram. This is not really necessary for a GCSE project. It is perfectly acceptable to produce an individual data flow diagram for each process to show where data comes from, where it is stored and how it moves around.

Task 5.1

Drawing a data flow diagram

After completing this task you should have drawn data flow diagrams to describe how data flows around the current system. To do this follow the steps listed below.

- Write a list of all the processes.
  For each process write a list of:

    — the inputs that are needed
    — the external entities that provide data for the process
    — the outputs that are produced
    — the external entities that receive data from the process
    — the data stores used by the process

- Open the Word file **DataFlowDiagrams.doc** (your teacher will provide this for you or it can be downloaded from the Student section at www.payne-gallway.co.uk). This file contains the data flow diagram symbols shown at the beginning of this chapter. You can use these symbols to draw your data flow diagrams.

- Follow the steps below to draw a data flow diagram for <u>each</u> process.

  - Draw and label a symbol for the process.
  - Draw and label all of the external entities that provide data for the process.
  - Draw and label all of the external entities that receive data from the process.
  - Draw and label all of the data stores that provide data for the process.
  - Draw and label all of the data stores that receive data from the process.
  - Connect the symbols with data flow arrows.
  - Label each data flow arrow to show which data is moving.
  - Check that you haven't drawn any data flow arrows directly between data stores and external entities. There should always be a process box in between to show what has happened to the data.

- Save your work using a sensible filename.

Chapter 6

Describing the possible solutions

To get a good mark for your project analysis you must describe and discuss some different ways of solving the problems you have identified. This shows that you considered alternative solutions before deciding how to solve the problem. Doing this will help you to justify your final choice of solution – we will look at how to do this in more detail in the next chapter. For now let's consider some of the possible alternative solutions that you might decide to write about.

- **Improve the existing system without using a computer**

  If the existing system is a manual filing system there are various ways that it might be improved without necessarily using a computer. In this case you should discuss at least one alternative manual system to the current one such as replacing card index boxes with filing cabinets.

- **Create a new system by writing a computer program**

  The advantage of this method is that a well-designed program would meet the needs of the user exactly. The main disadvantage of this method is that it can be time-consuming and expensive;

- **Create a new system by using an applications package**

  The advantage of this method is that commercially available software has already been thoroughly tested and can be installed quickly. Applications packages can also be customised to suit the needs of different users and provide solutions that are almost as good as a specially written program. This method of solution is also much less time-consuming than writing a computer program.

The discussion of possible solutions for the MovieZone system is shown on the next page.

Possible Solutions

Mr and Mrs Marshall could solve their information-handling problems by using a filing cabinet to store all their information about videos and members instead of using member and video details cards. The main advantage of this solution is that more information can be stored in a filing cabinet. The disadvantage of this solution is that information would still be based on paper records. These could easily be damaged, misplaced or lost just like the existing member and video details cards. It would also take just as much time to search through the filing cabinet to find information as it would to search through member or video details cards.

Another way of solving the problems would be to use a computer to store information about videos, members and loans. The advantages of this solution are that computers can store large amounts of data in a small space and search through it very quickly. The disadvantages of this solution are that computers can cost a lot of money and some of the MovieZone staff might not know how to use one. Some of them might find this very frightening and stressful.

There are two ways that a computer could be used. The first is to write a computer program to solve all of MovieZone's information-handling problems. The main disadvantages of this method are that I don't know how to write computer programs and Mr and Mrs Marshall can't afford to pay a programmer to do it. It can also be very expensive and time-consuming to write a computer program.

The next best alternative is to use an application package like a spreadsheet or a database. The application package could be set up to store and process all the information about videos, members and loans. Spreadsheets are good for solving problems that involve numbers and calculations. Databases are good for solving problems that involve storing and searching though information.

Task 6.1

Describing the possible solutions

After completing this task you should have described some possible solutions that could be used to solve the problems you have identified. To do this follow the steps listed over the page.

- Open the Word file **PossibleSolutions.doc** (your teacher will provide this for you or it can be downloaded from the Student section at www.payne-gallway.co.uk). You will see the template shown over the page.

Possible Solutions

[Put the name of the business, individual or organisation here] could solve their information-handling problems by [describe a way of solving the problems without using a computer here]. [Describe some advantages and disadvantages of this solution here].

Another way of solving the problems would be to use a computer to store information about [describe the information that would be stored here]. [Describe some advantages and disadvantages of using a computer here].

[Describe some different ways that a computer could be used to solve the problems here].

[Describe some advantages and disadvantages of these possible solutions here].

In the spaces provided on this template enter the information listed below. You can use the example given for the MovieZone project on page 38 to help. Remember to use ideas of your own using the example as a guide – don't just copy it out!

- First enter the name of the business, organisation or individual that you are carrying out the project for.

- Next describe a way of solving the problems without using a computer.

- Now describe some advantages and disadvantages of this solution.

- Next describe the information that would be stored if a computer was used to solve the problems. Go on to describe some general advantages and disadvantages of using a computer.

- Now describe some of the different ways that a computer could be used to solve the problems. Go on to describe some advantages and disadvantages of these possible solutions.

- Save your work using a sensible filename.

Chapter 7

Describing and justifying the chosen solution

After you have identified and discussed the possible solutions to the problems of your end-user you must decide which one you are going to use. You must give clear reasons to justify your choice of solution. The best way to do this is to describe the advantages of your chosen solution compared with the other possible solutions.

The description of the chosen solution for the MovieZone project is shown below.

Chosen Solution

The best way to solve the information-handling problems of MovieZone Video Rental will be to set up a new system using a computer. I have decided to use a computer because:

- computers can store large amounts of information in a very small space

- the information stored on a computer can be searched very quickly

- lists and reports about the information stored on a computer can be produced quickly and easily

- Mr and Mrs Marshall already have a computer

I have decided to do this using an application package because:

- I don't know how to write computer programs

- there are lots of different application packages that can be used to store and process information such as spreadsheet or database packages

- application packages can be customised to suit the needs of users and produce tailor-made solutions that are almost as good as writing a special computer program

- I have had a lot of experience using many different types of application packages in the past.

The most suitable type of application package will be a database because:

- database packages are specially designed to create computer-based files to store and process information in place of manual filing systems like the one that MovieZone are using at the moment

- I have used database packages before so I will be able to produce a much better system for MovieZone than if I use a type of package I know nothing about

- database packages can be customised to make using the system easier for the user, for example with data entry forms and menu screens. These are much easier to set up and use in a database rather than in a spreadsheet package.

Task 7.1

Describing and justifying the chosen solution

After completing this task you should have described the way that you have decided to solve the problems that were identified in the Problem Description. To do this follow the steps listed below.

- Open the Word file **ChosenSolution.doc** (your teacher will provide this for you or it can be downloaded from the Student section at www.payne-gallway.co.uk). You will see the template shown below.

Chosen Solution

The best way to solve the information-handling problems of [put the name of the business, individual or organisation here] will be to set up a new system using a computer. I have decided to use a computer because:

- [List the reasons for using a computer here]

I have decided to do this using an application package because:

- [List the reasons for using an application package here]

The most suitable type of application package will be a database because:

- [List the reasons for using a database package here]

In the spaces provided on this template enter the information listed below. You can use the example given for the MovieZone project on pages 40-41 to help but don't just copy what's there — your work must be your own so describe things in your own words and write down what <u>you</u> think.

- First enter the name of the business, organisation or individual that you are carrying out the project for.

- Next give the reasons for deciding to use a computer to solve the information-handling problems of your end-user.

- Now explain why you have chosen to use an application package to set up the new system.

- Finally give the reasons for using a database package.

- Save your work using a sensible filename.

Chapter 8

System objectives and performance criteria

It is important that you provide evidence throughout the analysis and design sections of your project that the users of the system have been consulted. Producing a set of **system objectives** is one way of doing this. It also sets out clearly the aims of the project. **Performance criteria** are used to identify how well your final solution solves the problems identified during the analysis stage of the project.

System objectives

System objectives are really just a list of the aims of the project written in simple plain English terms that your user can understand. These need to be shown to your user and agreed upon before you move on to the implementation stage. If you have agreed with the user on what needs doing at this stage it is much more likely that you will produce a system that does what they wanted it to in the end. The system objectives for the MovieZone system are shown below.

MovieZone System Objectives

The new system must be able to perform the following tasks:

- allow member details to be input, looked-up, edited and stored quickly, easily and accurately
- allow video details to be input, looked-up, edited and stored quickly, easily and accurately
- allow loan details to be input, looked-up, edited and stored quickly, easily and accurately
- allow video details to be searched to answer customer enquires quickly and easily
- produce a summary report listing member and video details for overdue videos
- produce reminder letters to members with overdue videos

Task 8.1

Describing the system objectives

After completing this task you should have described the objectives for your new system. To do this follow the steps listed below.

- Open the Word file **SystemObjectives.doc** (your teacher will provide this for you or it can be downloaded from the Student section at www.payne-gallway.co.uk). You will see the template shown below.

> ## System Objectives
> The new system must be able to perform the following tasks:
> - [List the tasks that the new system must be able to perform here]

- Click in the space provided next to the bullet point and type in the first of the system objectives for your project. This should be just one of the aims of the project written in straightforward non-technical language that your user will understand.

- Once you have written out the first system objective, press **Enter** and another bullet point will appear. Carry on like this until you have written out all of your system objectives.

- Save your work using a sensible filename.

- Print out a copy of the finished system objectives and check it for mistakes.

- Show your user the system objectives and make sure that they understand and agree them before you carry on. It is a good idea to get the end-user to sign the system objectives to show that you have consulted them and that they agree with what you are proposing to do.

Performance criteria

Good performance criteria should describe the **qualities** that the new system should have and the **quantities** that will be used to measure or demonstrate how successful it actually is. If you produce a clear, detailed set of performance criteria it will be very easy to gain high marks for the final evaluation of your project.

When describing the *qualities* of a system you should try to avoid being too general. Don't for example say things like, "the system should be easy to use". Be more specific with comments like, "new video records should be easy to enter" or "on-screen data entry forms should be clearly laid out".

When describing *quantities* you should give specific targets that are *measurable*. This might include statements like "the system must be able to store at least 30 video records" or "it should take no longer than 30 seconds to find a video record". Again, avoid being too vague. Statements such as "video records should be found quickly" don't really give us anything to aim for. How would you measure success in this case? What does 'quickly' mean – 10 seconds, 2 minutes, half an hour?

The performance criteria for the MovieZone system are shown below.

MovieZone Performance Criteria

The following criteria will be used to evaluate the success of the new system:

- the system must be able to store at least 10 member records
- the system must be able to store at least 25 video records
- the system must be able to store at least 10 loan records
- it must take no longer than 30 seconds to find and display a member, video or loan record
- it must take no longer than two minutes to answer customers' enquiries by entering search criteria and finding matching video records
- it must take no more than one minute to find and delete a member, video or loan record
- it must take no more than two minutes to find and edit a member, video or loan record
- it must take no more than two minutes to create a new member, video or loan record

- on-screen data entry forms must be clearly laid out to make data entry easy

- on-screen data entry forms must use automatic data validation to reduce data errors on input

- it must take no longer than 5 minutes to search for members with overdue videos and produce a summary report

- reminder letters to customers with overdue videos should be clearly laid out and include all the details of videos that need to be returned

Task 8.2

Describing the performance criteria

After completing this task you should have described the performance criteria for the new system. To do this follow the steps listed below.

- Open the Word file **PerformanceCriteria.doc** (your teacher will provide this for you or it can be downloaded from the Student section at www.payne-gallway.co.uk). You will see the template shown below.

Performance Criteria

The following criteria will be used to evaluate the success of the new system:

- [List the performance criteria for the new system here]

- Click in the space provided next to the bullet point and type in the first of the performance criteria for your project. This should be a *quality* that the new system must have or a *quantity* that will be used to measure how successful your final solution is.

- Once you have written out the first of the performance criteria press **Enter** and another bullet point will appear. Carry on like this until you have written out all of the performance criteria.

- Save your work using a sensible filename.

Chapter 9

Describing the current resources

You must describe any hardware and software already owned by your end-user. This is so that you can show this was taken into account before you decided exactly how to go about solving their information-handling problems. It may be that your user has a particular type of computer or software, and this may affect the way that you decide to solve the problem for them. You may also need to recommend upgrading hardware and purchasing new software, so it is important to know exactly what the user has at the moment.

It may be that the user doesn't have a computer. If this is the case you must find out exactly how much they are prepared to spend on buying new hardware and software. You'll need to describe exactly what they can buy for this amount of money. You can carry out some research into this by searching the Internet, reading advertisements or visiting a local computer shop if necessary. Remember to keep things sensible – don't start saying that your user has a budget of millions and will buy the latest Supercomputer!

The current resources for the MovieZone project are shown below.

MovieZone Current Resources

Mr and Mrs Marshall already have a computer with the following specification:

- Windows 95 operating system
- A Pentium II 200MHz processor
- 16Mb of RAM
- A 2Gb hard disk with 821Mb of free space
- A floppy disk drive
- A CD-ROM drive
- MS Office 97 Standard (this includes Word 97 and Excel 97)

Mr and Mrs Marshall can spend up to £1000 on new hardware and software if necessary.

Task 9.1

Describing the current resources

After completing this task you should have described the current resources of your own end-user. To do this follow the steps listed below. You may need to refer to information already collected from interviews and questionnaires.

Note: This task assumes that your end-user already has a computer. If they haven't you should say how much they could spend on new hardware and software.

Open the Word file **CurrentResouces.doc** (your teacher will provide this for you or it can be downloaded from the Student section at www.payne-gallway.co.uk). You will see the template shown below.

Current Resources

[Enter the name of the business, individual or organisation here] already has a computer with the following specification:

- [Enter the name of the operating system here] operating system
- [Enter the name of the processor here] [Enter the speed of the processor here] MHz processor
- [Enter the size of RAM here] Mb of RAM
- A [enter the size of hard disk (in Mb or Gb) here] hard disk with [enter the amount of free hard disk space (in Mb or Gb) here] of free space
- [List any other devices such as floppy disk drives and CD-ROM drives here]
- [List any applications software here]

[Say how much your end-user can spend on any new hardware and software here].

- Click in the spaces provided on the template and enter the information listed.
- Save your work using a sensible filename.

Part 2 – Design

This section covers the following topics:

Introduction

During the design stage you must produce a **system design specification** that describes the new system in detail. This should contain information about the following:

- the software that will be used to create the new system
- the hardware that will be needed to run the chosen software
- the data tables that will be needed
- data entry and menu form layouts
- the queries that will be needed to search the new database
- the reports that the new database must produce
- how the new system will be tested

Chapter 10

Relational databases

Many modern databases are **relational**. A relational database consists of one or more **tables**, which contain information about **entities**. An entity is simply one type of object or 'thing' such as a student in a school, a book in a library or a product for sale in a shop. The information about each individual entity is called a **record**. Records are divided up into **fields**. A field contains one individual item of data about an entity, such as the name of a student. Information about each type of entity is stored in a separate table. Tables are linked together by common fields. The links between tables are called **relationships**. Setting up relationships between tables avoids the duplication of data and makes it much easier to update the information in the database.

The example shown in Figure 10.1 below shows the tables that make up a relational database for a school library. Information is stored about students, books and loans – these are the **entities**. The book number and student number fields are used to link the tables together. So for example, even though a loan record does not contain the title of a book on loan this can be "looked up" in the Books table using the book number.

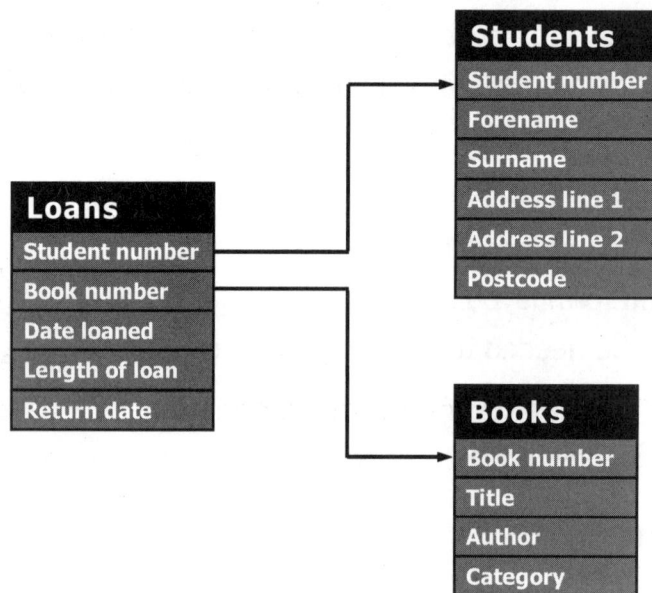

Figure 10.1: The structure of a relational database for a school library

Chapter 10
Relational databases

Designing a relational database

Every relational database is made up from a number of different parts. In Access 2000 these are called **objects**. The main object types you should consider when producing a design for an Access database are described below.

- **Tables**

  Tables are used to store information about entities in a database. You must think carefully about exactly what information needs to be stored about each entity – these individual bits of information are called **fields**. For every database table you must specify the fields that are required.

- **Queries**

  Queries are used to search through the information in a database to answer questions about it or make changes to it. You must decide what queries are needed. For each one you must say what it will be used for, why it is needed and which tables it will use. You must also choose the fields that will be displayed or changed.

- **Forms**

  On-screen forms are used to view and change information. A well-designed form will allow information to be entered or changed quickly and easily and help to reduce errors. You'll need to decide which forms are needed. For each one you must say which tables it will use, and choose the fields that will be displayed on it. You must also think carefully about the layout of each form and produce a hand-drawn design to show exactly how it should to look.

- **Reports**

  Reports are used to summarise and print out information. They are often used to display the information found by a query. For each report you must say which tables or queries it will use and choose the fields that are to be displayed on it. You must think carefully about the layout of each report and produce a hand-drawn design to show exactly how it needs to look.

- **Macros**

  Macros are used to perform tasks automatically by allowing complicated or repetitive processes to be carried out with the use of a single command. When designing a macro you must describe what it will do, what it will be called, where and when it will be used. List the individual steps or tasks that it needs to perform.

Exercise 10

1. Explain what is meant by the term **relational database**. (5)

2. What would each of the items listed below be used for in a relational database?
   (a) Queries (1)

   (b) Forms (1)

   (c) Reports (1)

   (d) Macros (1)

3. Suggest relationships that could be used to link the tables in the databases described below. In each case give **three** fields that would be needed in each table.

   (a) A small corner shop uses a database for stock control. The database consists of two tables. One table contains information about stock items. The other contains information about suppliers. (3)

   (b) A hotel uses a database to handle room bookings. The database consists of three tables. One table contains information about rooms. The second contains information about guests. The third table contains information about room bookings. (3)

4. An estate agent stores information about people who are selling houses. The information is kept on paper-based records in a filing cabinet.

   (a) Describe **two** tables that might be needed if a relational database was set up to replace the existing system. (2)

   (b) Give **four** fields that would needed in each table. You should explain what each field would be used for. (4)

   (c) Explain how these tables might be linked. (2)

Chapter 11

Choosing the software

During the analysis stage you decided to use a database application package to create the new system. The first stage of the design process is to decide which database package to use. To do this you need to compare the features offered by Access 2000 with those offered by at least one other database package. Once you have done this you must explain that Access 2000 is the best package to use because it offers all the features you need in order to set up the new system.

Other factors that you should also consider include what software your end-user already has, how much your end-user might be willing to spend on new software and how much experience of computers the people who will be using the system have. This last point is particularly important because inexperienced users will need a very friendly, easy-to-use system. This means that your chosen database package will need to have lots of features that allow you to customise it to match the needs of your end-users.

First let's consider the some of the features offered by Access 2000 that you might use when setting up a new database.

- A relational database can be created using common fields to link data tables

- On-screen data entry forms can be created and customised quickly and easily

- A wide variety of powerful query facilities can be used to search through data

- Sophisticated reports can be generated and formatted quickly and easily

- Links to other packages, such as to MS Word to generate standard letters, are possible

- Macros can be created and used to automate tasks, which can make a database much easier to use

- Menu screens can be set up to create tailor-made user interfaces that suit the needs of different groups of users

- Data tables can be 'locked' to prevent users from making changes by mistake

- Graphs and charts can be generated automatically to help with data analysis

The next step is to decide which database package you will compare with Access 2000. There are many database packages on the market and the features offered can vary widely from package to package, so it is impossible to consider them all here.

A good starting point is to think about a simpler database package that you might have used at school before starting GCSE. A typical example is **PinPoint**. This is a very good basic database package used in many schools by younger pupils to set up simple databases. It has lots of very useful features to help with the collection and analysis of data but can't be used to create relational databases. In addition to this some of the more advanced features offered by Access 2000 and other commercial database packages such as creating macros, generating and formatting reports and setting up customised menu screens aren't offered by PinPoint.

If you have had some experience using another basic database package it would be a good idea to compare this with Access 2000 when you discuss your final choice of software.

The choice of software for the MovieZone system is shown below.

Choice of Software

The database packages that I could use to set up the new system are PinPoint and Access 2000. These packages are available on the computers at school and my PC at home. Mr and Mrs Marshall don't have these packages on their computer but they are willing to spend up to £1000 on new hardware and software.

PinPoint offers the following features:

- Data can be entered easily using on-screen questionnaires

- Questionnaires can be designed and formatted quickly and easily

- The database is built up automatically behind the scenes as data is input

- Queries to search the database can be built up interactively and saved

- A wide variety of graphs and charts can be generated quickly and easily

- Data can be saved in a variety of file formats and used in other applications

Access 2000 offers the following features:

- Common fields can be used to link data tables and set up a relational database

- Data entry forms can be created and customised quickly and easily

- Powerful queries to search the database can be generated using wizards and saved

- Reports can be generated quickly using wizards and formatted very easily

- Tasks can be automated using macros

- An Access 2000 database can be linked to Word 2000 to generate mail-merge letters

- Customised menu screens can be created

I think that Access 2000 will be the best package to use for the new system because it will allow me to create a relational database. PinPoint does not offer this feature. Setting up a relational database will avoid the unnecessary duplication of data and make it much easier to update information. The staff of MovieZone don't have much experience with computers so the new system must be user-friendly. Access 2000 has more powerful features than PinPoint for customising a system, such as macros and menu screens, which can be used to make it more user-friendly. Mr and Mrs Marshall don't have Access 2000 on their computer but they have £1000 to spend on hardware and software so they can afford to buy it. Another important advantage is that I know how to use Access 2000 so it shouldn't take me too long to set up the new system.

Task 11.1

Describing the choice of software

After completing this task you should have described and justified your choice of software. To do this follow the steps listed below.

- Open the Word file **ChoiceofSoftware.doc** (your teacher will provide this for you or it can be downloaded from the Student section at www.payne-gallway.co.uk). You will see the template shown on the next page.

In the spaces provided on this template enter the information listed over the page. You can use the example just given for the MovieZone project to help but don't just copy what's there – your work must be your own, so describe things in your own words and write down what <u>you</u> think.

Choice of Software

The database packages that I could use to set up the new system are [put the name of the more basic database package here] and Access 2000. These packages are available on [say which computers these packages are available here].

[Put the name of the more basic database package here] offers the following features:

- [List some features of this database package here]

Access 2000 offers the following features:

- [List some features of Access 2000 here]

I think that Access 2000 will be the best package to use to set up the new system because [explain your reasons for choosing Access 2000 here].

- Enter the name of the more basic database package that you are going to consider in the space provided;

- Say which computers this package and Access 2000 are available on. These could include computers at school, your own PC if you have one and any computers that your end-user has. If your end-user doesn't have a computer or any of these database packages say here whether they can buy new software.

- List some features of the more basic database package. Include some features similar to ones found in Access 2000 and some that are different.

- List some features of Access 2000. Concentrate on the more advanced features that aren't found in the more basic database package.

- Finally give your reasons for choosing Access 2000. You should discuss the features offered by Access which you will need to use when setting up the new system, that aren't found in the more basic package.

- Save your work using a sensible filename.

Chapter 12

Describing the resource requirements

The resource requirements section of your project design must describe the hardware and software needed to set up and use the new system. You should start by listing the minimum specification of computer needed to run the software you have decided to use – in this case Access 2000.

To install and use Access 2000, a PC with the following specification is needed:

- Pentium processor or better with a speed of at least 75MHz
- Windows 95 or Windows 98 operating system
- at least 24Mb of RAM
- minimum of 161Mb of free hard disk space
- CD-ROM drive

You must compare this specification with the hardware that your user already has and decide whether any additional hardware or software is needed. You may need to recommend that your user should upgrade their existing hardware. Suppose for example that they have a computer with 16Mb of RAM. To run Access 2000 an additional 8Mb of memory is needed so you would have to recommend a memory upgrade and say how much it would cost. It might be that your user doesn't have a computer at all. In this case you should say how much they are prepared to spend on a new computer and describe what they will get for their money. In 2001 the standard specification for a PC costing approximately £750 was:

- Pentium III processor with a speed of 900MHz
- Windows ME operating system
- 128Mb of RAM
- 30Gb hard disk drive
- CD-ROM drive

This is more than enough to install and use Access 2000. Finally you should describe the hardware and software that is available for you to set up and test the new system either at home or at school.

The Resource Requirements for the MovieZone system are shown below.

MovieZone Resource Requirements

Access 2000 will be used to set up and run the new system for MovieZone. To install and use this software, a computer with the following minimum specification is needed:

- Pentium 75MHz processor or higher
- Windows 95 or later operating system
- minimum of 24Mb RAM
- at least 161Mb of free hard disk space
- CD-ROM drive

Mr and Mrs Marshall have a computer with the following specification:

- Pentium II 200MHz processor
- Windows 95 operating system
- MS Office 97 Standard (this includes Word 97 and Excel 97 but not Access)
- 16Mb of RAM
- 2Gb hard disk drive with 821Mb of free space
- CD-ROM drive
- floppy disk drive

Mr and Mrs Marshall have told me that they can spend up to £1000 on new hardware and software. I am going to recommend that they buy the Office 2000 Professional package, which includes Access 2000. This will cost £450. To install and run this software they will need to upgrade the memory in their computer from 16Mb to 24Mb. This will cost £40. Mr and Mrs Marshall will also need to buy a printer so that they can print out lists, reports and letters to members with overdue videos. I think a small laser printer will be the best choice because it will produce high quality printouts very quickly. This will cost approximately £350.

The computers at school and my PC at home all meet the minimum specification and already have Access 2000 installed. I will also need a printer. Every computer room at school has a laser printer so this isn't a problem. I also have a small inkjet printer at home that I can use. This means that I have all the resources I need to set up and test the new system.

Task 12.1

Describing the resource requirements

After completing this task you should have described the hardware and software resources that will be needed to set up and operate your new system. To do this follow the steps listed below.

- Open the Word file **ResourceRequirements.doc** (your teacher will provide this for you or it can be downloaded from the Student section at www.payne-gallway.co.uk). You will see the template shown below.

Resource Requirements

Access 2000 will be used to set up and run the new system for [put the name of the business, individual or organisation here]. To install and use this software a computer with the following minimum specification is needed:

- [List the minimum specification of computer needed to run Access 2000 here]

[Describe the hardware and software your user already has here].

[Describe any extra hardware or software your user will need here].

[Describe the hardware and software available for you to set up and test the new system at home and school here].

- Enter the name of the business, individual or organisation in the first space provided.

- Next list the minimum specification of a computer needed to run Access 2000.

- If your end-user already has a computer, describe its specification in the space provided. If they don't have a computer, use this space to say so.

- If your end-user already has a computer but it doesn't meet the minimum specification needed to run Access 2000, describe what must be done to upgrade it. If your end-user doesn't have a computer, or has one that can't be upgraded, you should describe the type of computer that they will need to buy and say how much it will cost.

- Finally, describe the hardware and software available for you to set up and test the new system at home and school.

- Save your work with a sensible filename.

Chapter 13

Describing the new system

At the start of the design section you should produce a **system overview**. This must describe the new system in terms of the input, processing and output that will take place. A typical system overview will contain information about:

- the data that will be input
- when data will be input
- how data will be input
- the processing that will be needed
- the information that will be output
- when information will be output
- how information will be output
- the data that will be stored
- where data will be stored
- the type of user interface that will be needed

The system overview for the MovieZone system is shown below.

MovieZone System Overview
Input

Data will be input about members, videos and loans. This data will be input when:

- a new member joins
- an existing member's details change
- a new video is bought
- an existing video's details change
- a video is rented
- a video is returned
- members ask questions about videos

This information will be input manually using a keyboard and on-screen data entry forms.

Processing

Data will be processed when:

- new member details need to be saved
- changes to an existing member's details need to be saved
- new video details need to be saved
- changes to an existing video's details need to be saved
- rental details need to be saved when a video is rented
- rental details need to be deleted when a video is returned
- videos matching a member's enquiries need to be found
- details of members with overdue videos need to be found
- letters to members with overdue videos need to be generated

Output

Information will be output on screen when:
- member details are looked up
- video details are looked up
- videos matching a member's enquiries are found

Information will be printed when:
- details of members with overdue videos are found
- letters to members with overdue videos are generated

Data stores

Data about members, videos and loans will be stored on the hard disk drive of the computer.

User interface

The user interface will be menu-based. This will limit the choices available and make the system easier for inexperienced users to use.

Task 13.1

Preparing a system overview

After completing this task you should have written a description of the main parts of your new system. To do this follow the steps listed below.

- Open the Word file **SystemOverview.doc** (your teacher will provide this for you or it can be downloaded from the Student section at www.payne-gallway.co.uk). You will see the template shown below.

System Overview

Input

Data will be input about [describe the input data here]. This data will be input when:

- [describe when this data will be input here]

This information will be input using [describe how this data will be input here].

Processing

Data will be processed when:

- [describe the processing that will take place here]

Output

Information will be output on screen when:

- [describe when data will be output on screen here]

Information will be printed when:

- [describe when data will be printed here]

Data stores

Data about [list the data that will be stored here] will be stored on [list the storage devices that will be used here].

User interface

[describe the type of user interface that will be needed here].

- Complete the template by clicking in the highlighted areas and typing the required information.

- Save your work using a sensible filename.

Chapter 14

Designing tables

The first stage in designing any relational database is to identify the entities that information needs to be stored about. Information about each type of entity should be stored in a separate table. Detailed designs for the tables must then be produced to specify exactly what data needs to be stored in them about each different type of entity. A table design should include the following information about each field:

- **Field name**

  This is what the field is going to be called. A table that stores information about students, for example, might have fields with names like Surname, Forename, Address and Date-of-Birth.

- **Data type**

  The data type that should be used for a field depends on what you want to store in it. Some of the different data types available in Access 2000 are described below.

Text	This data type allows text or a mixture of text and other characters including numbers to be stored in a field. It is used to store things like names, addresses and postcodes. Up to 255 characters can be stored in a text field.
Number	This data type is used to store data in fields that contain just numbers. This can be a **byte** for numbers between 0 and 255, **integer** for whole numbers between −32,768 and 32,767, **long integer** for large whole numbers and **decimal** for numbers with decimal points in them.

Autonumber
This data type is often used for **primary** or **key fields**. It automatically inserts a unique number in a field when a new record is created. The number inserted is always next in sequence from the last one. So if a record was created and Autonumber put the value 1 in the field, the next value to be inserted when another record was created would be 2 and so on.

Currency
This data type is used to store numbers that represent amounts of money.

Boolean
This data type only allows the values **Yes/No** or **True/False** to be stored in a field.

Date/time
This data type is used to store dates or times.

Memo
This data type allows large amounts of text to be stored in a field. It is used to store things like descriptions and notes. Up to 64,000 characters can be stored.

- **Validation rule**

Validation rules are used to check data as it is being entered to make sure that it is **allowable** and **sensible**. Data that is not sensible or allowed should be rejected and an appropriate message displayed for the user. It is very important that you describe and set up some validation rules. Checking that these work will form an important part of both your test plan and test results. Using validation rules helps to prove that a new system can handle **normal**, **extreme** and **erroneous data** – we'll say more about this in Chapter 27.

To decide on the validation rule for a field you must think about the possible values that it can have. If a field is numeric it might be that only numbers in a certain range are allowed, such as 0 to 100 for examination marks, or 7 to 11 for the year groups in a high school. Text fields can also contain certain values such as M or F to represent 'male and 'female' for gender. Some fields may contain a wide range of possible values. For example a field storing addresses could contain many different values. In cases like this you must say that a validation check just isn't possible.

- **Description**

    Each field should have a short description about the sort of data it will store. Suppose we have a field called Forename in a student data table. The description for this field might be something like, "This is the first name of the student".

- **Typical data**

    For each field, an example should be given of a typical value it might contain. Typical data for a Date-of-Birth field might, for example, be given as 05-04-87.

Designing tables for the MovieZone system

During the analysis we found out that the MovieZone video rental shop stored information about members, videos and loans. These are the entities for this system. This tells us that we're going to need three tables in the new database to store information about each entity. The detailed designs for these tables are shown on the next two pages.

Table: Members

Field Name	Data Type	Validation Rule	Description	Typical Data
MemberNo	Number	Must be between 1 and 5000	Number used to identify a member	1019
FirstName	Text	None – any value possible	First name of member	Mark
Surname	Text	None – any value possible	Surname of member	Porter
AddressLine1	Text	None – any value possible	First line of member's address	21 Green Lane
AddressLine2	Text	None – any value possible	Second line of member's address	Talke
Town	Text	None – any value possible	Town that the member lives in	Stoke-on-Trent
County	Text	None – any value possible	County that the member lives in	Staffordshire
Postcode	Text	None – any value possible	Postcode of member's address	ST8 9LP
DateOfBirth	Date	Must be a valid date	Date of birth of member	22/11/81

The **primary key** for this table is **MemberNo**.

Table: Videos

Field Name	Data Type	Validation Rule	Description	Typical Data
VideoNo	Number	Must be between 1 and 1000	Number used to identify a video	1092
Title	Text	None – any value possible	The title of the video	Star Wars
Category	Text	Must be one of Act, Com, Hor, Scf, Thr	The category of the video	SCF
Certificate	Text	Must be one of U, 12, PG, 15, 18	The certificate of the video	U

The **primary key** for this table is **VideoNo**.

Table: Loans

Field Name	Data Type	Validation Rule	Description	Typical Data
MemberNo	Number	Must be on Members table	Number used to identify a member	1019
VideoNo	Number	Must be on Videos table	Number used to identify a video	1092
LengthofLoan	Number	Can only be 1, 2 or 3	How many days the video has been loaned out for	2
DateDue	Date	Must be greater than current date and no more than three days ahead	The date the video is due to be returned	21/06/01

The **primary key** for this table is **VideoNo**.

Task 14.1

Designing the tables for your project

This task involves designing the tables for your GCSE project. You should have worked carefully through this chapter before attempting it. You will need to keep the completed table designs safe until you're ready to start setting up your project database.

- Open the Word file **TableDesign.doc** (your teacher will provide this for you or it can be downloaded from the Student section at www.payne-gallway.co.uk). You will see the template shown below.

Table: [write the name of the table here]

Field Name	Data Type	Validation Rule	Description	Typical Data

The **primary key** for this table is [write the name of the **primary key** here].

- Enter the name of the first table that you're going to design in the space provided.
- Enter the name of the first field for this table in the empty box underneath the heading **Field Name**.
- Click in the box underneath **Data Type** and enter the data type for this field.
- Click in the box underneath **Validation Rule** and enter the validation rule for this field. Remember if a field can't be validated you should enter, "None – any value possible".
- Click in the box underneath **Description** and enter a short description about the data that this field is going to store.
- Click in the box underneath **Typical Data** and enter an example of typical data for this field.
- Click on the **Tab** key to create a new blank row and repeat the above process for the next field.

Click in the space provided underneath the table and enter the name of the field that will be the **primary key**. This is the field that must have a unique value for each record in the table. For example in the **Videos** table we chose **VideoNo** as the primary key because every copy of a video is given its own unique number to identify it.

- Save your work using a sensible filename.

- Repeat all of these steps until you have Word files containing individual designs for each table. Keep these designs safe because you'll need to refer to them later on when you set up your own database.

Chapter 15

Describing the relationships between tables

We have already seen that a relational database consists of one or more **tables**, which contain information about **entities**. Tables are linked together by common fields and the links between them are called **relationships**. In this chapter we will look at how to describe the relationships between the entities in different tables. This is an important part of the design process because it describes exactly how tables should be linked to each other when a database is being created.

Types of relationship

Relationships are often described using an **entity-relationship diagram**. Entities can be related to each other in one of three ways. These are explained below along with their corresponding entity-relationship diagrams.

- **One-to-one**
  E.g. Headteacher and school. A headteacher is in charge of one school, and a school has one headteacher.

  | Headteacher |——————————————| School |

- **One-to-many**
  E.g. Form and student. A form has many students but a student belongs to just one form.

  | Form |————————————<| Student |

- **Many-to-many**
  E.g. Teacher and student. A student has many teachers, and each teacher teaches many students.

  | Teacher |>————————————<| Student |

Drawing an entity-relationship diagram

To draw an entity-relationship diagram you should work through the steps listed below. Don't expect to get it right first time! You'll probably need to draw a diagram in rough a few times before producing a final version.

- Identify the entities. You should have done this earlier when you described the tables that would be needed (remember each entity is represented by **one** table).
- Draw **one** box for each entity.
- Show the relationships between entities by drawing lines to connect the boxes together.
- Use arrows at the ends of the lines to show the type of relationship (one-to-one, one-to-many, many-to-many).

Entity-relationship diagrams for the MovieZone system

The **Member table** will be linked to the **Loan table** using the **Member number** field. This is a **one-to-many** relationship because each member can rent many videos. This is shown in the entity-relationship diagram below.

The **Video table** will be linked to the **Loan table** using the **Video number** field. This is a **one-to-one** relationship because a video can only be on loan to one member at a time, and a loan refers to only one video. This is shown in the entity-relationship diagram below.

These relationships could be represented together in a single diagram as shown in Figure 15.1.

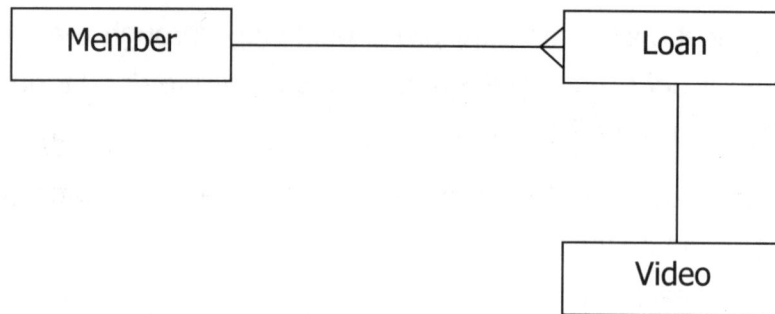

Figure 15.1: Entity-relationship diagram for the MovieZone system

Exercise 15

Draw entity-relationship diagrams to illustrate the relationships described below.

(a) One driver can drive only one car at a time.

(b) A pop group has one lead singer supported by a number of other group members.

(c) A teacher teaches one class containing many students.

(d) A school contains many students who each study many subjects.

(e) The Olympic Games have a number of different events each of which has many athletes competing in them.

(f) A library contains many books and has a lot of members who can each borrow more than one book at a time.

(g) An airline flies to many destinations. Only one aircraft flies to a destination at a time but it carries many passengers.

Task 15.1

Drawing entity-relationship diagrams

After completing this task you should have described in words the relationships between the entities in the new database and drawn entity-relationship diagrams to illustrate them.

- Open the Word file **EntityRelationships.doc** (your teacher will provide this for you or it can be downloaded from the Student section at www.payne-gallway.co.uk). You will see the template shown below.

- Complete the description in words to explain how the table will be linked to other tables.

- Draw an entity-relationship diagram by drawing **one** box for each entity, drawing lines to connect the boxes and show the relationships between the entities, using arrows at the ends of the lines to show the type of relationship.

Entity-relationship diagram

The [write the name of the first table here] table will be linked to the [write the name of the second table here] table using the [write the name of the common field that will be used to link these tables here] field. This is a [write the type of relationship here] relationship because [explain why this type of relationship is needed between these tables here]. This is shown in the entity-relationship diagram below.

[Draw the entity-relationship diagram here].

- When you've completed the template for a table and drawn the entity-relationship diagram to go with it, save the file with a sensible filename.

- Repeat all of these steps for each table.

- You could combine your diagrams to produce a single entity-relationship diagram like the one shown in Figure 15.1 – this isn't essential provided you've clearly described the relationships for each table.

Chapter 16

Designing data entry forms

We have already seen that **data entry forms** are used in a relational database to view and change the information in **tables**. Well-designed forms allow information to be entered or changed quickly and easily and help to reduce errors. In this chapter we will look at how to design data entry forms.

The first step is to think about the data that must be input into the new system. To do this you must look back at your table designs – these contain detailed descriptions of all the data that will be input and stored in the database. In general at least one data entry form will be needed for each table in a database. In the MovieZone system we decided that data will be stored about members, videos and loans in three tables. This tells us that three data entry forms are needed – one for each table.

The next step is to think about exactly what needs to go on each form. Some of the items that are commonly found on data entry forms are described below. You will need to decide which of these needs to be included on each of the forms that you design.

- **Fields**

  Deciding which fields to include is the most important step of the form design process. You need to decide which table the form will be used to input data for and exactly which fields from this table need to be on it. You should only include the fields that are needed. If data for a particular field doesn't need to be input on a form don't include it. Putting unnecessary fields on a form can confuse users and make it look cluttered and untidy.

- **Text labels**

  Text labels are used to put headings and instructions for users on a form. You should normally include a text label with a name for the form that tells users what it is used for. Text labels can also be used to give users help on how to fill in a form.

- **Pictures**

  Pictures can be included on a form to make it more attractive. They can also help to inform the user about what the form is used for. In a library system, for example, a picture of a book could be included on a data entry form that is used to add, edit and delete book details.

- **Command buttons**

  Command buttons are often used to make a database more user-friendly by allowing actions such as browsing through the records in a table, creating new records or deleting existing records to be carried out by clicking on them. Command buttons can also be used to link forms with menu screens to help users find their way around a database more easily. For example a command button could be included on a data entry form to take the user back to the Main menu screen when it is clicked. We will look at how to design menu screens in the next chapter.

- **Combo boxes**

  Combo boxes are used to find records by allowing users to enter a value or choose from a list. In a library system the details for a book could be found by offering the user a drop-down list of book numbers to choose from. When a book number is selected the details for that book will be found and displayed.

You must prepare a hand-drawn design for each data entry form showing every item that will need to appear on the form. When designing data entry forms try to make their layout as user-friendly and attractive as possible. Some tips to help you do this are listed below.

- Use clear, easy-to-read fonts for text such as Times New Roman or Arial.

- Space objects out evenly and line them up.

- Make sure the layout of each form is consistent with other forms.

The data entry form designs for the MovieZone system are shown over the next few pages.

Data entry form design for: **frmMembers**

This form will be used to find, add, edit and delete member details.

This form will use fields from the following table(s):

Table name	Field(s)
tblMembers	MemberNo, FirstName, Surname, AddressLine1, AddressLine2, Town, County, Postcode, DateOfBirth

Members ← Arial 26 pt, bold.

Find member with membership no   (NB. Standard background)

combo box (member no)

Address Line 1

Address Line 2

Town

County

Postcode

(first) (previous) (next) (last) (add) (delete)

Member Number

First Name

Surname

Date Of Birth

(All text labels and boxes Arial 11 pt.
Text labels only
bold)

Main Menu (open frmMainMenu)

Arial 12 pt, bold.

Data entry form design for: **frmVideos**

This form will be used to find, add, edit and delete video details.

This form will use fields from the following table(s):

Table name	Field(s)
tblVideos	VideoNo, Title, Category, Certificate

Videos
Arial 26 pt, bold.

(NB. Standard <u>background</u>)

Find video with video number

→ combo box (videoNo)

Video Number

Title

Category

Certificate

(All text labels and boxes
Arial 11 pt. Text labels
<u>only</u> bold.)

(first) (previous) (next) (last) (add) (delete)

Find Videos
(open frm FindVideos)
Arial 12 pt bold.

Main Menu
(open frmMain Menu)
Arial 12 pt, bold.

Data entry form design for: frmLoans

This form will be used to find, add, edit and delete loans details.

This form will use fields from the following table(s):

Table name	Field(s)
tblMembers	FirstName, Surname, AddressLine1, AddressLine2, Town, County, Postcode
tblLoans	VideoNo, LengthofLoan, DateDue

Loans — Arial 26 pt, bold.

Find loans for member number ▼ combo box (member no)

(NB. Standard background)

Surname

(first) (previous) (next) (last)

Overdue — Arial 12 pt, bold

Main Menu — Arial 12 pt, bold

(Delete) (Add)

(All text labels and boxes Arial 11 pt. Text labels only bold)

First Name

Address Line 1

Address Line 2

Town

County

Postcode

Video No

Length of Loan ☐ days

Date Due

Task 16.1

Designing data entry forms

After completing this task you should have produced data entry form design sheets for your own database project.

- Open the Word file **FormDesign.doc** (your teacher will provide this for you or it can be downloaded from the Student section at www.payne-gallway.co.uk). You will see the template shown on the next page.

Complete this template by entering the information listed below. Use the examples on pages 78-80, which show data entry form designs for the MovieZone system.

- First enter a name for the data entry form.
- Enter a sentence to say what the form will be used for.
- Enter the name of the tables containing the fields that the form will display.
- List the fields that will be displayed from each table next to the table name.
- Design the layout of the form in the rest of the space on the template. You should show the position of fields, text labels (including font type and size), command buttons and the names of any macros linked to them, pictures and any dividing lines.
- Save your work using a sensible filename.

Repeat this process until you have produced a design for each data entry form needed in your new system.

Data entry form design for: frm[enter the name of the form here]

This form will be used to [describe what this form will be used for here].

This form will use fields from the following tables/queries:

Table/query name	Field(s)
[Enter the field or query name here]	[List the fields from this table/query that will be used on the form here]

[Design the layout of the form in this space]

Chapter 17

Designing queries

Queries are a very flexible and powerful tool in Access 2000. They can be used to search a database to find records matching certain conditions, generate forms or reports, update tables and analyse data.

To decide on the types of queries required by a database you must refer back to the system objectives and performance criteria. Look for any situations where the database will need to be searched to find records matching certain conditions. Ignore cases where individual records simply need to be looked up, such as finding the details for a member by entering their membership number – we have already found that this can be done quickly and easily on a form. Working through this process for the MovieZone system tells us that queries are needed to do the following:

- Search the Videos table to find videos matching customers' criteria such as:

  Videos with the same **Certificate**

  Videos with the same **Category**

  Videos with the same **Certificate** and **Category**

  A video with a certain **Title**

- Search the Loans table to find overdue videos. This query will be used to generate an Overdue Videos report and mail-merged reminder letters for members with overdue videos.

You should produce a detailed design for each query that describes what it will search for, the tables that it will search and the fields that will be displayed or changed.

The designs for the MovieZone queries are shown on the next page.

Query: Videos

This query will use the **Videos table** to search for records matching the following conditions:

- Every video with a particular **Certificate** e.g. "18"

- Every video in a particular **Category** e.g. "Hor"

- Every video with a particular **Certificate** and **Category** e.g. "18" and "Hor"

- Every video with a particular **Title** e.g. "The Skulls"

These fields need to be displayed for the records that are found:

- **VideoNo**
- **Title**
- **Category**
- **Certificate**

These records need to be sorted into **ascending** order of **VideoNo**.

Query: Overdue

This query will use the **Members**, **Videos** and **Loans** tables to search for records matching the following condition:

- Every video on loan with a **DateDue** less than the current date.

These fields need to be displayed for the records that are found:

- **First Name**
- **Surname**
- **Address Line 1**
- **Address Line 2**
- **Town**
- **County**
- **Postcode**
- **VideoNo**
- **Title**
- **DateDue**

These records need to be sorted into **ascending** order of **MemberNo**.

Task 17.1

Designing queries

After completing this task you should have produced designs for the queries needed in your project database.

- Open the Word file **QueryDesign.doc** (your teacher will provide this for you or it can be downloaded from the Student section at www.payne-gallway.co.uk). You will see the template shown below.

Query: [write the name of the query here]

This query will use the [give the name of the table(s) that this query must search through to find records that match the search condition(s)] table to search for records matching the following condition(s):

- List the search conditions that this query will use to find matching records

These fields need to be displayed for the records that are found:

- List all of the fields that must be displayed for matching records

These records need to be sorted into [write either **ascending** or **descending** here] order of [give the name of the field that will be used to sort the records into this order]

Enter the information listed below in the spaces provided on the template.

- Enter a name for the query.
- Enter the names of the tables that this query will search through to find records.
- Enter the search conditions that this query will use to find matching records.
- List all of the fields that must be displayed for matching records.
- Finally write either **ascending** or **descending** to describe the order that matching records need to be sorted into and give the name of the field that will be used to sort the records.

Repeat this process for each query.

- Save your work using a sensible filename.

Chapter 18

Designing reports

Forms are used to enter data and view records on screen. When information needs to be printed, **reports** should be used. This is because forms usually contain coloured text, backgrounds and graphics that do not print very well, and usually show only one record.

To decide on the types of report required by a database you must refer to the system objectives and performance criteria. Look for any situations where information needs to be printed – for example records found by a query often need to be printed out. Working through this process for the MovieZone system tells us that just one report is needed to print the information found by the overdue videos query.

You should prepare a hand-drawn design for each report. This must describe the tables or queries that the information will come from, the fields that need to be included, and the way that the report should be laid out and formatted.

The design for the Overdue Videos report for the MovieZone system is shown on the next page.

Report design for: rptOverdue

This report will be used to display information about all of the videos that are overdue.

This report will use fields from the following tables/queries:

Table/query name	Field(s)
qryOverdue	MemberNo, FirstName, Surname, AddressLine1, AddressLine1, Town, County, Postcode, VideoNo, Title, DateDue

Overdue Videos ← Arial 20 pt, bold.

Surname → bold text for these two fields.

(NB. Border around field boxes transparent)

(Text for all fields shown Arial 9 pt.)

FirstName

AddressLine1

AddressLine2

Town

County

Postcode

VideoNo Title (Arial 10 pt, bold)

Date Due

(date) (Arial 10 pt, bold)

(page number) (Arial 10 pt, bold)

Designing reports

After completing this task you should have produced designs for the reports needed in your project database.

- Open the Word file **ReportDesign.doc** (your teacher will provide this for you or it can be downloaded from the Student section at www.payne-gallway.co.uk). You will see the template shown over the page.

Complete this template by entering the information listed below. Use the example on page 92, which shows the overdue report for the MovieZone system.

- First enter a name for the report.
- Next enter a sentence to say what the report will be used for.
- Now enter the name of the tables or query that the report will display information from.
- List the fields that will be used on the report.
- Design the layout of the report in the rest of the space on the template. You should show the position of fields, headings and other text labels (including font type and size), page numbers, dates and any dividing lines.
- Save your work using a sensible filename.

Repeat this process until you have produced a design for each report needed in your new system.

Report design for: rpt[enter the name of the report here]

This report will be used to [describe what this report will be used for here]

This report will use fields from the following tables/queries:

Table/query name	Field(s)
[Enter the table or query name here]	[List the fields from this table/query that will be used on the report here]

[Design the layout of the report in this space]

Chapter 19

Designing menu forms

Menus help to make a system easier to use by limiting the choices available to users, which reduces the chance of them making mistakes. One way to create a menu in Access 2000 is to use a blank form and put command buttons on it. Command buttons can be placed on a form and set up to perform actions when the user clicks on them. For example a command button could be set up to open a form, run a query or print a report when clicked.

You must first produce an overall design for the menu system showing how the different menus will be linked together. The overall menu design for the MovieZone system is shown in Figure 19.1 below.

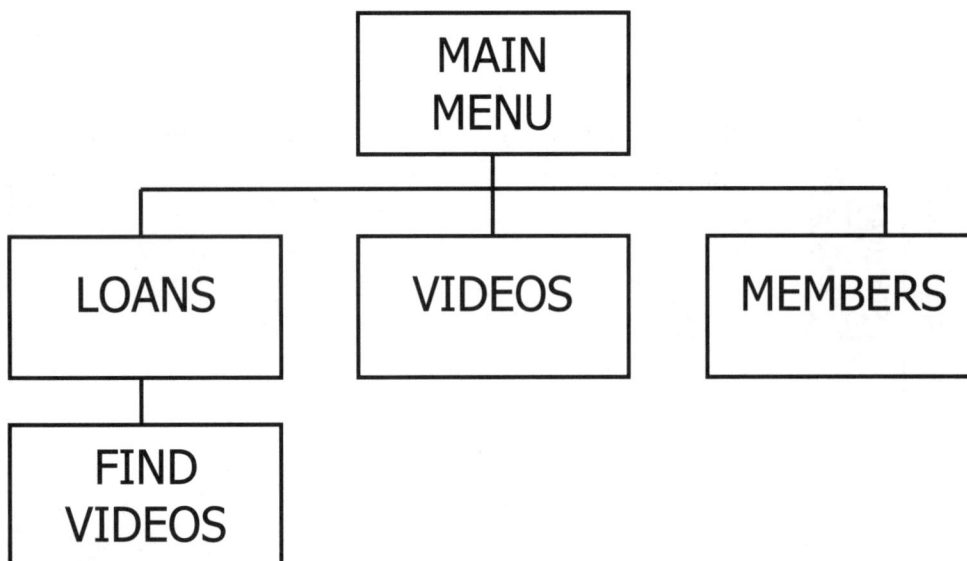

Figure 19.1: The overall menu design for the MovieZone system

In the example above a Main menu links three data entry forms together – Loans, Videos and Members. A Find Videos menu is linked to the Loans form – this will be used to offer the user various search options and run queries when they are selected.

Task 19.1

Producing an overall menu design

After completing this task you should have produced an overall menu design for your own database project.

- Open the Word file **OverallMenuDesign.doc** (your teacher will provide this for you or it can be downloaded from the Student section at www.payne-gallway.co.uk).

- Choose **View**, **Toolbars**, **Drawing** from the Menu bar.

- Use the text box tool ▤ to draw boxes to represent menu screens and data entry forms.

- Join the boxes together by drawing lines with the line tool ╲

- Save your work with a sensible filename when you have finished.

You must also produce detailed hand-drawn designs for each menu shown on the overall menu design. The individual menu designs for the MovieZone system are shown on the next two pages.

Menu form design for: frmMainMenu

This menu will be used to display the main options available to users of the MovieZone system.

(NB. Standard background)

Movie Zone ← Arial 48 pt, italic, bold.

Main Menu ← Arial 36 pt, bold.

Loans	Videos	Members
(open frmLoans)	(open frmVideos)	(open frmMembers)

Quit
(quit application)

(All text on command buttons Arial 18 pt, bold.)

Menu form design for: **frmFindVideosMenu**

This menu will be used to display the options available for searching the information in the Videos table of the MovieZone system.

(NB. Standard background)

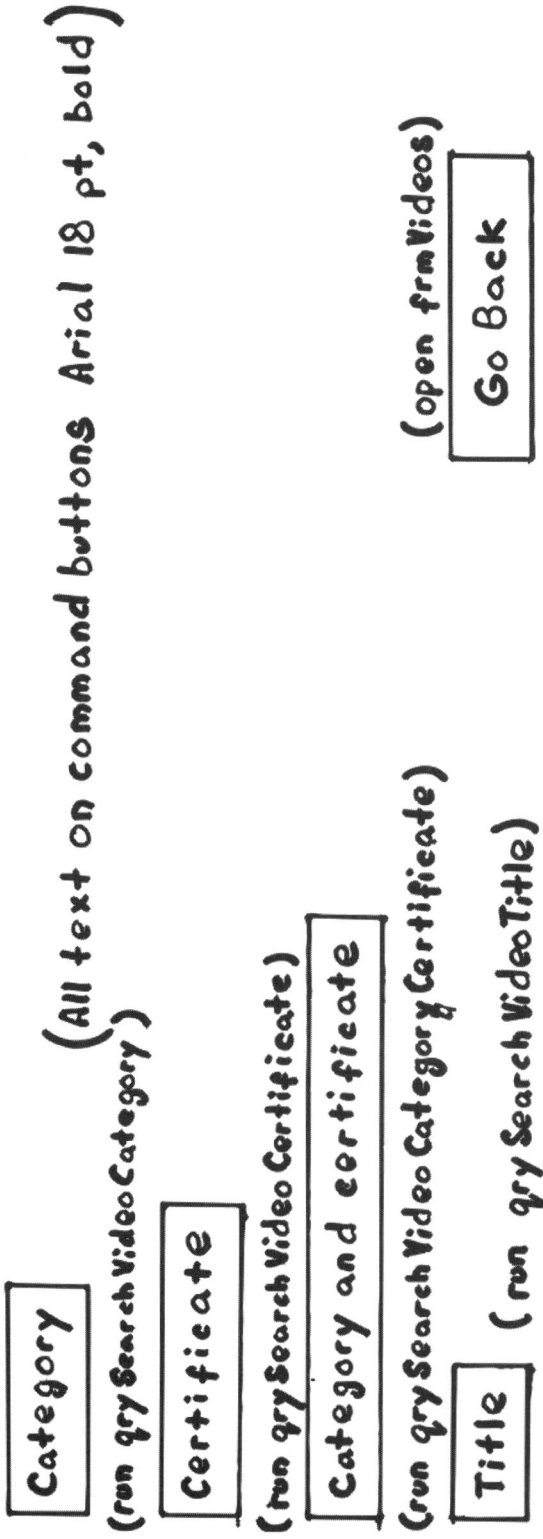

Find Videos ← Arial 26 pt, bold.

(All text on command buttons Arial 18 pt, bold)

Category
(run qrySearchVideoCategory)

Certificate
(run qrySearchVideoCertificate)

Category and certificate
(run qrySearchVideoCategory&Certificate)

Title (run qrySearchVideoTitle)

(open frmVideos)

Go Back

Task 19.2

Designing menu forms

After completing this task you should have produced menu form design sheets for your own database project.

- Open the Word file **MenuDesign.doc** (your teacher will provide this for you or it can be downloaded from the Student section at www.payne-gallway.co.uk). You will see the template shown on the next page.

Complete this template by entering the information listed below. You can use the examples on pages 90 and 91, which show the menu form designs for the MovieZone system to help.

- First enter a name for the menu.
- Next enter a sentence to say what the menu will be used for.
- Design the layout of the menu in the rest of the space on the template. You should show the position of command buttons and the names of any menus or forms they will open, text labels pictures and dividing lines. You should also specify the background to be used, font types and sizes for all text and indicate where any colour is needed.
- Save your work using a sensible filename.

Repeat this process until you have produced a design for each menu form needed in your new system.

Menu form design for: **frm**[enter the name of the form here]

This menu will be used to [describe what this menu will be used for here]

[Design the layout of the menu form in this space]

Chapter 20

Preparing a test plan

Many GCSE projects lose marks unnecessarily because they have been poorly tested. This is often because the **test plan** is incomplete or even missing altogether. A test plan describes the tests that must be carried out to make sure a new system works correctly and satisfies both the system objectives and performance criteria.

To get a good mark for testing your project you must prepare a detailed test plan and produce evidence to show that all of the tests were actually carried out. This chapter describes how to prepare a test plan. We will look at how to carry out the tests and discuss the evidence that needs to be collected in Chapter 31.

Contents of a test plan

A test plan is normally presented in a table like the one shown below.

Test No	Purpose of test	Test data	Expected result

The following items should be entered in the table for each test:

- **Test No**

  Giving each test its own unique number makes it much easier to refer to specific tests when you write the final evaluation for the project. Do this by simply starting at 1 and counting up.

- **Purpose of test**

  This should be a short description of what the test is for. Or, in other words, what you are trying to prove. Remember each test must be carried out for a clear reason linked to the system objectives or performance criteria. Suppose for example one of the performance criteria for a new student records database was, "it must take no more than one minute to find and delete a student record". The purpose of a test to prove that the new system can do this might be something like, "Delete student record".

- **Test data**

   Test data are the actual values that will be input in order to carry out a test. For the example of the student records database above, the test data might be "Delete record for student number 1010". This assumes of course that there is already a record in the database for student number 1010. This may sound obvious but it is always worth checking!

   For some tests – such as making sure that a command button works by clicking on it – no data will need to be input. In such cases it is best to just describe what needs to be done such as, "click on Quit button".

   The tests described in the test plan must aim to find out if the new system can handle **normal**, **extreme** and **erroneous** data. These three types of test data are described below.

   - **Normal** test data is used to check that a system can handle the sort of data that would be expected during day-to-day use;

   - **Extreme** test data is used to check that a system can cope with data that lies on the boundaries of what is acceptable;

   - **Erroneous** (or exceptional) test data is used to check that a system can identify data that is wrong and reject it;

   Figure 20.1 over the page shows part of a test plan with these three types of test data. The tests shown are being used to check part of a system that will be used to input student examination marks in the range 0 to 100.

   Test 1 uses **normal** test data to check that the system will accept marks within the allowed range.

   Tests 2 and 3 use **extreme** test data to check that the system will accept marks on the boundaries of the allowed range – in this case 0 and 100.

   Test 4 uses **erroneous** test data to check that the system will reject marks outside the allowed range.

Test Nº	Purpose of test	Test data	Expected result
1	Test input mark function for marks within the allowed range	Enter a mark of 50	Mark accepted
2	Test input mark function for marks on the lower limit of the allowed range	Enter a mark of 0	Mark accepted
3	Test input mark function for marks on the upper limit of the allowed range	Enter a mark of 100	Mark accepted
4	Test input mark function for marks out of the allowed range	Enter a mark of 101	Mark rejected

Figure 20.1: Testing normal, extreme and erroneous conditions

- **Expected result**

  This should explain what should happen when a test is actually carried out.

The complete test plan for the MovieZone system is shown over the next few pages. The tests shown fall into one of the five main categories listed below.

1. Tests to show that information can be added, edited and deleted.
2. Tests to show that validation checks work and can handle normal, extreme and erroneous data.
3. Tests to show that queries find the correct information in tables.
4. Tests to show that reports list the right information in the correct format.
5. Tests to show that command buttons on menus and data entry forms do what they're supposed to do when a user clicks on them.

Exercise 20

Work through the test plan for the MovieZone system shown on pages 97-103. Decide which of the above categories each test falls into. Write 1, 2, 3, 4 or 5 next to each test on a copy of the test plan. Your teacher will give you this or it can be downloaded from the Student section at www.payne-gallway.co.uk.

MovieZone Test Plan

Test Nº	Purpose of test	Test data	Expected result
1	To test that a new member record can be added to the Members table	See below	New record added to Members table
2	To test that the details in an existing member record can be changed	Change AddressLine1 for MemberNo 101 to '19 Crowther Street'	Details to record changed and saved in Members table
3	To test that an existing record can be deleted from the Members table	Delete record for MemberNo 113	Record removed from Members table
4	To show that the details for an existing member record can be found and displayed on the Members form	Display the Members form, click on the down-arrow of the 'Find member number' combo box, choose '112' in the list	Details for MemberNo 112 are found and displayed on the form
5	To test that a new video record can be added to the Videos table	See below	New record added to Videos table
6	To test that the details in an existing video record can be changed	Change Title for VideoNo 122 to 'Highlander 2 – The Quickening'	Details to record changed and saved in Videos table
7	To test that an existing record can be deleted from the Videos table	Delete record for VideoNo 119	Record removed from Videos table
8	To show that the details for an existing video record can found and displayed on the Videos form	Display the Videos form, click on the down-arrow of the 'Find video number' combo box, choose '106' in the list	Details for VideoNo 106 are found and displayed on the form
9	To test that a new loan record can be added to the Loans table	See below	New record added to Loans table
10	To test that the details in an existing loan record can be changed	Change Title for MemberNo 122 to 'Highlander 2 – The Quickening'	Details to record changed and saved in Loans table

Test No	Purpose of test	Test data	Expected result
11	To show that the details of all videos on loan to a particular member can be found and displayed on the Loans form	Display the Loans form, click on the down-arrow of the 'Find loans for member number' combo box, choose '111' in the list	Details of videos on loan to MemberNo 111 are found and displayed along with their personal details
12	To test that an existing record can be deleted from the Loans table	Display the Loans form, click on the down-arrow of the 'Find loans for member number' combo box, choose '109' in the list, delete the loan details for VideoNo 106	Record removed from Loans table
13	Check that normal data can be entered in the VideoNo field of the Videos table	Enter the value '500' in the VideoNo field	Value accepted
14	Check that extreme data can be entered in the VideoNo field of the Videos table	Enter the value '1' in the VideoNo field	Value accepted
15	Check that extreme data can be entered in the VideoNo field of the Videos table	Enter the value '1000' in the VideoNo field	Value accepted
16	Check that erroneous data cannot be entered in the VideoNo field of the Videos table	Enter the value '1500' in the VideoNo field	Error message displayed
17	Check that normal data can be entered in the Category field of the Videos table	Enter the value 'Hor' in the Category field	Value accepted
18	Check that erroneous data cannot be entered in the Category field of the Videos table	Enter the value 'Car' in the Category field	Error message displayed
19	Check that the correct values are displayed in the drop-down list box for the Category field on the Videos form	Click on the down-arrow of the drop-down list box for the Category field on the Videos form	Only the values 'Act', 'Com', 'Hor', 'Scf' and 'Thr' should be displayed in the list

Test Nº	Purpose of test	Test data	Expected result
20	Check that normal data can be entered in the Certificate field of the Videos table	Enter the value 'PG' in the Certificate field	Value accepted
21	Check that erroneous data cannot be entered in the Certificate field of the Videos table	Enter the value '11' in the Certificate field	Error message displayed
22	Check that the correct values are displayed in the drop-down list box for the Certificate field on the Videos form	Click on the down-arrow of the drop-down list box for the Certificate field on the Videos form	Only the values 'U', '12', 'PG', '15' and '18' should be displayed in the list
23	Check that normal data can be entered in the MemberNo field of the Members table	Enter the value '2500' in the MemberNo field	Value accepted
24	Check that extreme data can be entered in the MemberNo field of the Members table	Enter the value '1' in the MemberNo field	Value accepted
25	Check that extreme data can be entered in the MemberNo field of the Members table	Enter the value '5000' in the MemberNo field	Value accepted
26	Check that erroneous data cannot be entered in the MemberNo field of the Members table	Enter the value '6500' in the MemberNo field	Error message displayed
27	Check that normal data can be entered in the LengthofLoan field of the Loans table	Enter the value '2' in the LengthofLoan field	Value accepted
28	Check that erroneous data cannot be entered in the LengthofLoan field of the Loans table	Enter the value '7' in the LengthofLoan field	Error message displayed
29	Check that extreme data can be entered in the LengthofLoan field of the Loans table	Enter the value '1' in the LengthofLoan field	Value accepted
30	Check that extreme data can be entered in the LengthofLoan field of the Loans table	Enter the value '3' in the LengthofLoan field	Value accepted

Test N°	Purpose of test	Test data	Expected result
31	Check that normal data can be entered in the DateDue field of the Loans table	Enter a date 2 days ahead of the current date in the DateDue field	Value accepted
32	Check that erroneous data cannot be entered in the DateDue field of the Loans table	Enter a date 4 days ahead of the current date in the DateDue field	Error message displayed
33	Check that erroneous data cannot be entered in the DateDue field of the Loans table	Enter 31/02/2002 in the DateDue field	Value not accepted
34	Check that extreme data can be entered in the DateDue field of the Loans table	Enter a date 3 days ahead of the current date in the DateDue field	Value accepted
35	To test that the video table can be searched to find all videos in the same category	Choose 'Find videos by category' on the Search Videos menu screen and enter 'Hor' when asked for a category	4 records found and displayed
36	To test that the video table can be searched to find all videos with the same certificate	Choose 'Find videos by certificate' on the Search Videos menu screen and enter '15' when asked for a certificate	9 records found and displayed
37	To test that the video table can be searched to find all videos with the same category and certificate	Choose 'Find videos by category and certificate' on the Search Videos menu screen, enter 'Com' when asked for a category and enter '15' when asked for a certificate	3 records found and displayed
38	To test that the video table can be searched to find videos with a certain title	Choose 'Find videos by title' on the Search Videos menu screen and enter 'The Skulls' when asked for a title	1 record found and displayed

Test N°	Purpose of test	Test data	Expected result
39	To test that the Loans table can be searched to find overdue videos	Double-click on the Overdue query in the queries list of the Database window	7 records found and displayed
40	To show that a report listing the member and video details for all overdue videos can be printed	Click on the Overdue button on the Loans form	Overdue videos report is printed out
41	To show that reminder letters to members with overdue videos can be printed	Open the overdue letter in MS Word and click on the Print Merge button	Reminders letters for 5 members are printed out
42	To test that the Main menu is displayed when the database is opened	Click on the MovieZone icon on the desktop	The MovieZone database is opened and the Main menu is displayed
43	To test that the Videos form is displayed when the Videos button on the Main menu is clicked	Click on the Videos button on the Main menu	The Videos form is displayed
44	To test that the Members form is displayed when the Members button on the Main menu is clicked	Click on the Members button on the Main menu	The Members form is displayed
45	To test that the Loans form is displayed when the Loans button on the Main menu is clicked	Click on the Loans button on the Main menu	The Loans form is displayed
46	To test that the system shuts down when the Quit button on the Main menu is clicked	Click on the Quit button on the Main menu	The system is shut down
47	To test that the Find Videos menu is displayed when the Find Videos button on the Videos form is clicked	Click on the Find Videos button on the Videos form	The Find Videos menu is displayed
48	To test that the Videos form is displayed when the Go Back button on the Find Videos menu is clicked	Click on the Go Back button on the Find Videos menu	The Videos form is displayed

Test Nº	Purpose of test	Test data	Expected result
49	To test that the Main menu is displayed when the Main Menu button on the Videos form is clicked	Click on the Main Menu button on the Videos form	The Main menu is displayed
50	To test that the Main menu is displayed when the Main Menu button on the Members form is clicked	Click on the Main Menu button on the Members form	The Main menu is displayed
51	To test that the Main menu is displayed when the Main Menu button on the Loans form is clicked	Click on the Main Menu button on the Loans form	The Main menu is displayed
52	To test that the first record in the Videos table is displayed when the First Record button on the Videos form is clicked	Click on the First Record button on the Videos form	The first record in the Videos table is displayed
53	To test that the last record in the Videos table is displayed when the Last Record button on the Videos form is clicked	Click on the Last Record button on the Videos form	The last record in the Videos table is displayed
54	To test that the next record in the Videos table is displayed when the Next Record button on the Videos form is clicked	Click on the Next Record button on the Videos form	The next record in the Videos table is displayed
55	To test that the previous record in the Videos table is displayed when the Previous Record button on the Videos form is clicked	Click on the Previous Record button on the Videos form	The previous record in the Videos table is displayed
56	To test that a new blank record is created and displayed when the New Record button on the Videos form is clicked	Click on the New Record button on the Videos form	A new blank record for the Videos table is created and displayed
57	To test that the current record is deleted when the Delete Record button on the Videos form is clicked	Click on the Delete Record button on the Videos form	A message warning that a record is about to be deleted is displayed

Test Nº	Purpose of test	Test data	Expected result
58	To test that the first record in the Members table is displayed when the First Record button on the Members form is clicked	Click on the First Record button on the Members form	The first record in the Members table is displayed
59	To test that the last record in the Members table is displayed when the Last Record button on the Members form is clicked	Click on the Last Record button on the Members form	The last record in the Members table is displayed
60	To test that the previous record in the Members table is displayed when the Previous Record button on the Members form is clicked	Click on the Previous Record button on the Members form	The previous record in the Members table is displayed
61	To test that a new blank record is created and displayed when the New Record button on the Members form is clicked	Click on the New Record button on the Members form	A new blank record for the Members table is created and displayed
62	To test that the current record is deleted when the Delete Record button on the Members form is clicked	Click on the Delete Record button on the Members form	A message warning that a record is about to be deleted is displayed
63	To test that the current record is deleted when the Delete Record button on the Loans subform is clicked	Click on the Delete Record button on the Loans subform	A message warning that a record is about to be deleted is displayed

New record details for Test Nº 1

MemberNo	115
FirstName	Gavin
Surname	Pryke
AddressLine1	91 Brook Drive
AddressLine2	Brookfield
Town	Alsager
County	Cheshire
Postcode	CH12 9UB
DateOfBirth	18/6/72

New record details for Test Nº 5

VideoNo	125
Title	The Fly
Category	Hor
Certificate	18

New record details for Test Nº 9

MemberNo	110
VideoNo	115
LengthofLoan	2
DateDue	*current date + 2*

Task 20.1

Preparing a test plan

After completing this task you should have prepared a test plan for your database.

- Open the Word file **TestPlan.doc** (your teacher will provide this for you or it can be downloaded from the Student section at www.payne-gallway.co.uk). You will see the table shown below.

Test No	Purpose of test	Test data	Expected result

- Enter the details of the first test in the empty row. When you have finished this press the Tab key to generate a new empty row. Carry on entering your tests in this way until the test plan is complete.

- Now check your work – have you:

  included tests covering each of the categories listed below?

  1. Tests to show that information can be added, edited and deleted.
  2. Tests to show that validation checks work and can handle normal, extreme and erroneous data.
  3. Tests to show that queries find the correct information.
  4. Tests to show that reports list the right information in the correct format.
  5. Tests to show that command buttons on menus and data entry forms do what they're supposed to do when a user clicks on them.

  entered the **Test No**, **Purpose**, **Test Data** and **Expected Result** for each test?

- Save your work with a sensible filename.

Part 3 – Implementation

This section covers the following topics:

Introduction

The implementation stage involves setting up the system described in the design specification. This will involve:

- preparing a **system implementation plan**
- setting up the system as specified in the design
- producing an **implementation commentary** to describe how you:

    created and linked data tables
    created and customised data entry forms
    set up queries
    created reports
    created and linked menus

Chapter 21

Documenting the system implementation

Implementation involves setting up the system described in the design specification. To get a good mark for implementation you must provide evidence of the work that has been carried out by including a **system implementation plan** and an **implementation commentary** in your project report. This chapter explains what these items are and how to prepare them. We'll look at the system implementation plan first.

System implementation plan

A system implementation plan should list the tasks you will need to complete in order to set up the system. This should be prepared before you do anything. The system implementation plan for the MovieZone system is shown below.

MovieZone System Implementation Plan

To set up the MovieZone system I must complete the following tasks:

1. Create a new blank database
2. Create a table to store information about members
3. Create a table to store information about videos
4. Create a table to store information about loans
5. Set up relationships to link the members, videos and Loans tables together
6. Create a data entry form for the Members table
7. Create a data entry form for the Videos table
8. Create a data entry form for the Loans table
9. Create a query to search the Videos table for all videos with a certain category
10. Create a query to search the Videos table for all videos with a certain certificate
11. Create a query to search the Videos table for all videos with a certain category and certificate
12. Create a query to search the Videos table for all the videos with a certain title
13. Create a query to search the Loans table for videos that are overdue
14. Create a report to print information about overdue videos
15. Create a menu form to display the Main menu options
16. Create a menu form to display the find video options

17. Prepare a mail-merge document that can be used in a to generate personalised reminder letters for members with overdue videos

Task 21.1 below describes how to prepare a system implementation plan for your project.

Task 21.1

Preparing a system implementation plan

After completing this task you should have produced designs for the reports needed in your project database.

- Open the Word file **ImplementationPlan.doc** (your teacher will provide this for you or it can be downloaded from the Student section at www.payne-gallway.co.uk.) You will see the template shown below.

System Implementation Plan

To set up the [enter the name of the system here] system I must complete the following tasks:

- [List the tasks that must be completed here]

Complete this template by entering the information listed below. You can use the example given in this chapter for the MovieZone system to help.

- Enter the name of the system in the first space provided.

- Type in the first of the tasks that must be completed in the next space. Once you have done this, press **Enter** and another number will appear. Carry on like this until you have listed all of the tasks.

- Save your work using a sensible filename.

Implementation commentary

Your implementation commentary should describe the features of the software that you used to complete the tasks listed in the system implementation plan. You should try to keep descriptions in this section short and illustrate them with screenshots or printouts whenever appropriate. It is best to build up an implementation commentary as you actually create the new system. You should not try to produce a software manual for Access 2000. Some examples from the implementation commentary for the MovieZone system are shown below.

Task 1

Creating a new database

To create the MovieZone Videos database I loaded Access 2000, clicked in the **Blank Access Database** checkbox and clicked on **OK** (see opposite).

I entered the filename **MovieZone** and clicked on **Create** (see below).

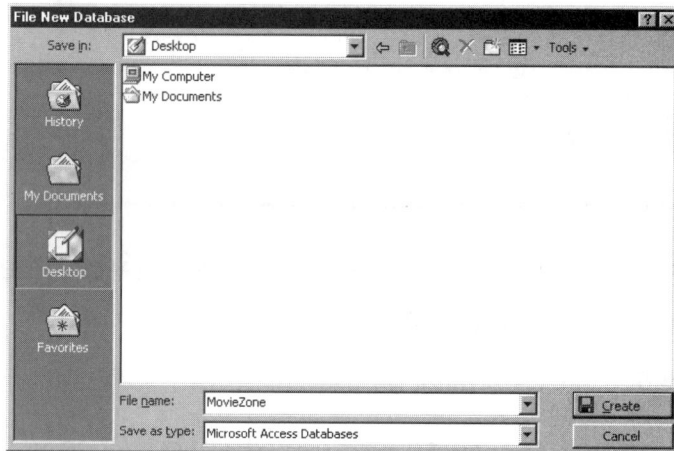

Task 2

Creating the Members table

To create the Members table I completed the steps listed below.

- Clicked on the **Table** in the Database window.
- Double-clicked on **Create table in Design View**.
- Entered the field names and data types so that they were the same as those shown in the design for the Members table (see below).

Field Name	Data Type	Description
MemberNo	Number	
FirstName	Text	
Surname	Text	
AddressLine1	Text	
AddressLine2	Text	
Town	Text	
County	Text	
Postcode	Text	
DateOfBirth	Date/Time	

- Made **MemberNo** the key field by clicking in the **MemberNo** row and choosing **Edit**, **Primary Key** from the menu.

- Saved the table design with the filename **tblMembers**.

The rest of the chapters in this section describe in detail how to carry out the system implementation for the MovieZone system. The implementation commentary for your project does not have to be this detailed. You must, however, make sure that you explain clearly exactly what you did and include evidence such as screenshots and printouts of forms, queries, reports etc. to prove it.

Chapter 22

Creating a new database and tables

In this chapter you will learn how to load Access, create a new database and set up data tables. These are the first basic steps that must be followed in order to start developing a relational database in Access 2000.

Loading Access

Exactly how you load Access will depend on whether the computer you are working on is at home or in school. There may be an Access icon on the screen (Figure 22.1), which you can click on. Alternatively you may need to click on **Start** in the bottom left-hand corner of the screen and choose **Programs**, **Microsoft Access** (Figure 22.2).

Figure 22.1: The Access icon

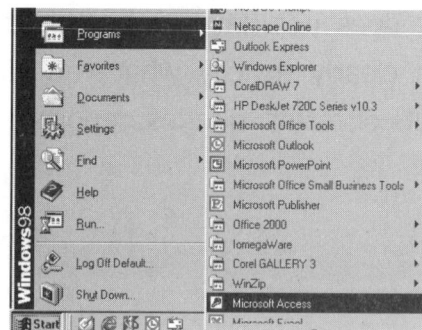

*Figure 22.2: The **Start** menu*

Task 22.1

Creating a new database

This task describes how to use Access 2000 to create the new MovieZone Videos database.

- Load Access.

- Select the **Blank Access Database** checkbox and click on **OK** (Figure 22.3).

Figure 22.3: Creating a new database

- Type in the filename **MovieZone** and click on **Create** (Figure 22.4).

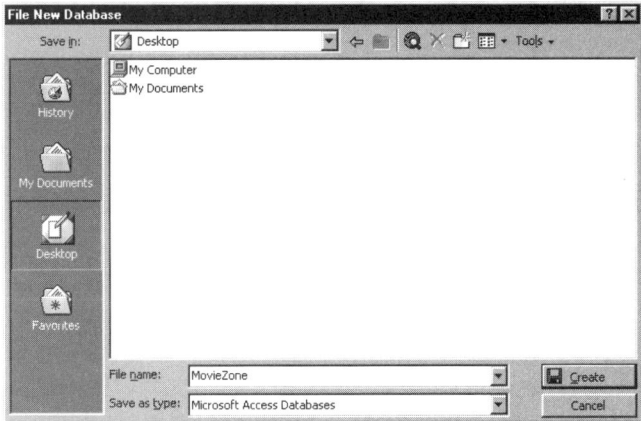

Figure 22.4: Naming a new database

A window with the heading **MovieZone : Database** at the top will appear – this is called the Database window (Figure 22.5). Every database created in Access 2000 has a Database window just like this one, which will appear whenever it is opened. The Objects bar lists the different types of object such as tables, queries, forms and reports that a database can contain.

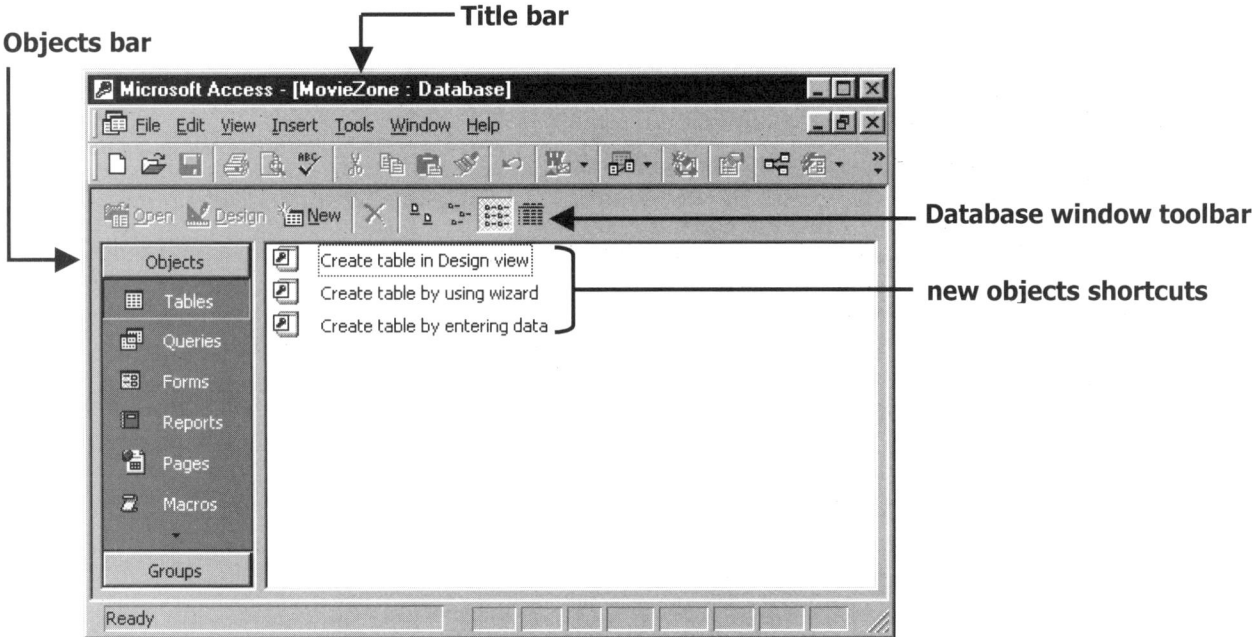

Figure 22.5: The Database window

Clicking on an object name in the Objects bar will list all the objects of that type that are currently in the database. Clicking on an item in the Objects bar, then double-clicking on an object shortcut, will create a new object. The Database window contains an icon that will switch to Design View so that objects can be changed. This window also contains icons that can be used to open existing objects or create new ones.

Task 22.2

Setting up the Members table

This task describes how to set up the Members table for the MovieZone database. Once this table has been created, data can be entered and stored in it.

- Start in the Database window.

- Click once on the **Table** object type.

- Double-click the **Create table in Design View** icon. A blank table like the one shown opposite in Figure 22.6 will appear in which you can enter the fields you need for a table.

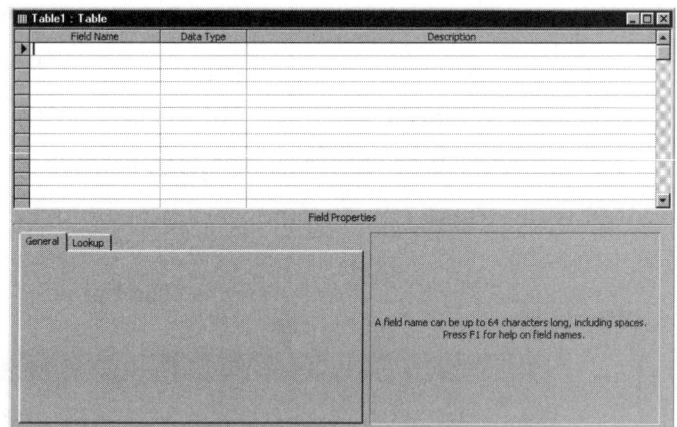

Figure 22.6: Table Design View

- In the **Field Name** column type the **field names** listed below — these are exactly the same as those shown in the Members table design on page 66.

> **MemberNo**
> **FirstName**
> **Surname**
> **AddressLine1**
> **AddressLine2**
> **Town**
> **County**
> **Postcode**
> **DateOfBirth**

Next we need to make sure that the **data types** for each field are the same as those specified in the table design. Unless the data type for a field is changed it will be automatically set as **Text** by Access 2000 – this is the **default data type**.

In the design for the Members table all the fields except for **MemberNo** and **DateOfBirth** are **Text** so we only need to change data types for these two fields.

- To choose **Number** as the data type for the **MemberNo** field click in the **Data Type** column next to **MemberNo** and click the small down-arrow on the right-hand side of this box. You will see a drop-down list of data types – click on **Number**.
- Choose **Date/Time** as the data type for **DateOfBirth** in exactly the same way.

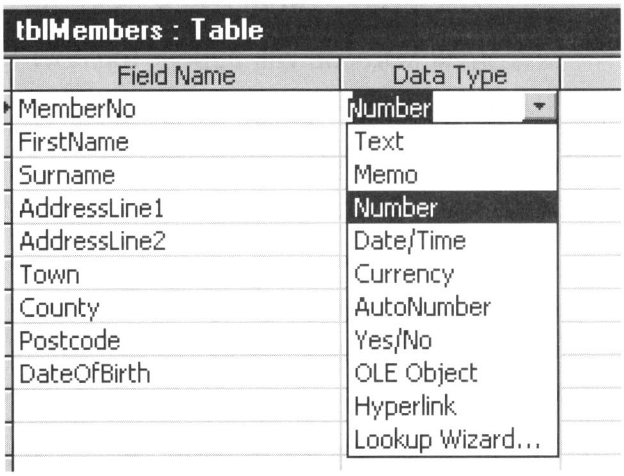

Figure 22.7: Changing the data type for a field

The table design should now look exactly like the one shown below in Figure 22.8.

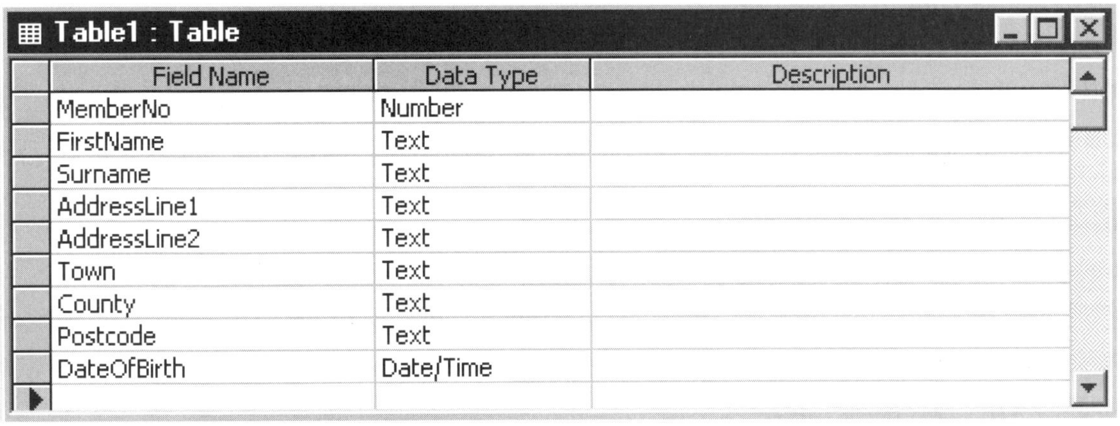
Table1 : Table

Field Name	Data Type	Description
MemberNo	Number	
FirstName	Text	
Surname	Text	
AddressLine1	Text	
AddressLine2	Text	
Town	Text	
County	Text	
Postcode	Text	
DateOfBirth	Date/Time	

Figure 22.8: The completed Members table shown in Design View

Next we need to choose a **key field** for this table. A key field is used to uniquely identify a record. In this case the key field is **MemberNo** because every member of MovieZone is given their own individual membership number when they join. This stops members being mixed up with each other if for example they have the same name.

- Click in the **MemberNo** row.
- Choose **Edit**, **Primary Key** from the menu.

  A small key icon will appear to show that this field is now the **primary key** for each record in this table.

Finally we need to save the new table and give it a name.

- Click the **X** in the top right-hand corner of the table design window.
- You will see the message shown in Figure 22.9 below – click on **Yes** to save changes.

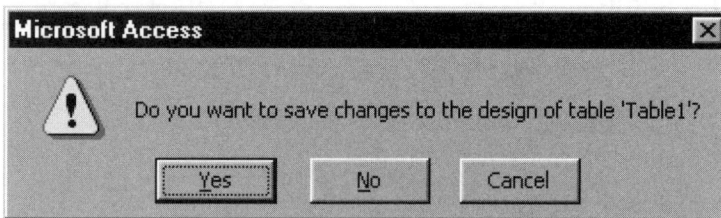

Figure 22.9: Saving the changes to a table

- Another window will appear asking you to enter a table name (Figure 22.10). Type **tblMembers** and click on **OK**.

Figure 22.10: Naming a table

You have now created the Members table. Next you will create the tables for Videos and Loans in exactly the same way. We'll deal with the Videos table first.

Task 22.3

Setting up the Videos table

This task describes how to set up the Videos table for the MovieZone database.

- Start in the Database window.

- Click once on the **Table** object type and double-click on the **Create table in Design View** icon.

- In the **Field Name** column type in each of the **field names** listed below – these are exactly the same as those shown in the Videos table design on page 66.

> **VideoNo**
> **Title**
> **Category**
> **Certificate**

- Next make sure that the **data types** for each field are the same as those shown in the table design. Do this in exactly the same way as described earlier in Task 22.2.

- The **key** field for this table is **VideoNo** because every copy of a video at MovieZone is given its own individual number. This stops different copies of the same video being mixed up with one another.

  Click in the **VideoNo** row and choose **Edit**, **Primary Key** from the menu.

You should have now created the Videos table. The completed table design should look exactly the same as the one shown in Figure 22.11 below – if it doesn't, make any necessary corrections before saving it.

	Field Name	Data Type	Description	
🔑	VideoNo	Number		
	Title	Text		
	Category	Text		
	Certificate	Text		
▶				

tblVideos : Table

Figure 22.11: The completed Videos table shown in Design View

- Click the **X** in the top right-hand corner of the Table Design window.
- Click on **Yes** to save changes.
- Type **tblVideos** and click on **OK**.

Task 22.4

Setting up the Loans table

This task describes how to set up the Loans table for the MovieZone database.

- Start in the Database window.
- Click once on the **Table** object type and double-click on the **Create table in Design View** icon.
- In the **Field Name** column type in each of the **field names** listed below – these are exactly the same as those shown in the Loans table design on page 67.

> **MemberNo**
> **VideoNo**
> **LengthofLoan**
> **DateDue**

- Next make sure that the **data types** for each field are the same as those shown in the table design. Do this in exactly the same way as described earlier in Task 22.2.

The **key field** for this table is **VideoNo** because each video can only be rented to one member at a time.

- Click in the **VideoNo** row and choose **Edit**, **Primary Key** from the menu.

The completed table design should look exactly the same as the one shown in Figure 22.12 – if it does not, make any necessary corrections before saving it.

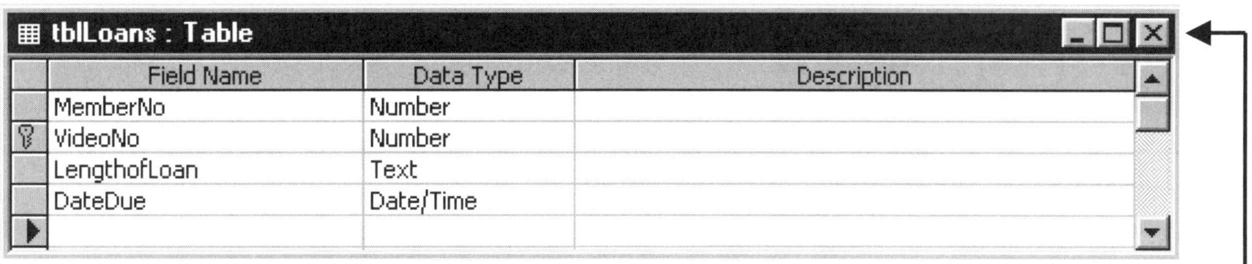

Field Name	Data Type	Description
MemberNo	Number	
VideoNo	Number	
LengthofLoan	Text	
DateDue	Date/Time	

tblLoans : Table

Figure 22.12: The completed Loans table shown in Design View

- Click the **X** in the top right-hand corner of the Table Design window.

- Click on **Yes** to save changes.

- Type **tblLoans** and click on **OK**.

Chapter 23

Linking tables

Once the tables for a relational database have been created they must be linked together. This chapter describes how to link the Members, Videos and Loans tables created for the MovieZone system in the previous chapter.

Task 23.1

Creating links between tables

Tables are linked in Access by creating **relationships** between them – these relationships were described in the design section using **entity-relationship diagrams**. The Members, Videos and Loans tables must be displayed in the **Relationships window** before relationships can be created to link them.

- Select **Tools**, **Relationships** from the Menu bar (Figure 23.1).

Figure 23.1: Creating relationships to link tables

The **Show Table** window will appear as shown in Figure 23.2 with the **Relationships window** behind it.

- We'll add the **Members table** first — it doesn't really matter in what order you add tables to the Relationships window as long as you can see all the tables that need linking.

- Click once on **tblMembers** and **Add**.

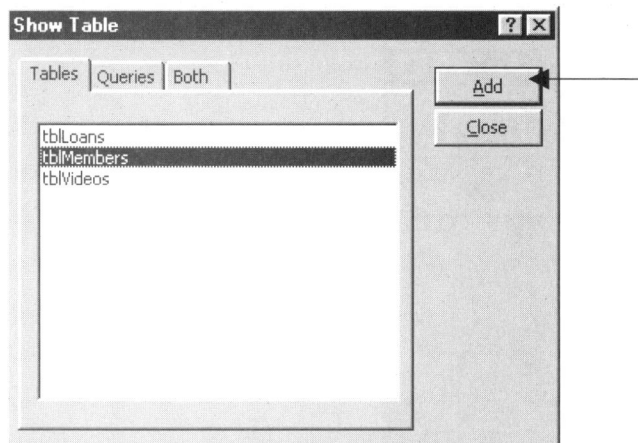

Figure 23.2: The Show Table window

- Click once on **tblLoans** and **Add**.

- Click once on **tblVideos** and **Add**.

- Click on **Close**.

All three tables should now be displayed in the relationships window as shown in Figure 23.3 below.

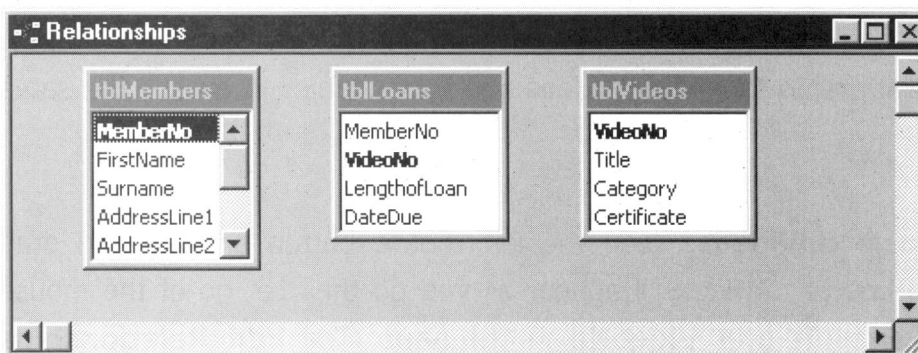

Figure 23.3: Tables displayed in the relationships window

- Click on **MemberNo** in **tblMembers**. Keep the left mouse button pressed and drag across towards **tblLoans**. A line will appear as you do this. Let go of the mouse button when the arrow is over **MemberNo** in **tblLoans**. The **Edit Relationships** window will appear (Figure 23.4).

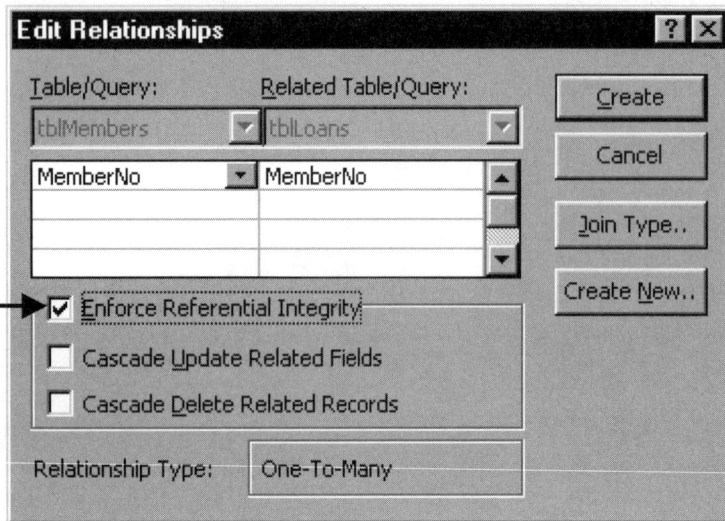

Figure 23.4: Editing a relationship

- Click the **Enforce Referential Integrity** box.
- Click **Create**. A line showing the link between the tables will appear. This link is defined as a **One-To-Many** relationship because *one* member can have *more than one* video on loan at a time.

Next we'll create a relationship to link the Videos and Loans tables in exactly the same way.

- Click on **VideoNo** in **tblVideos**. Keep the left mouse button pressed and drag across towards **tblLoans**. A line will appear as you do this. Let go of the mouse button when the arrow is over **VideoNo** in **tblLoans**. The **Edit Relationships** window will appear.
- Click the **Enforce Referential Integrity** box.
- Click **Create**. This time the link is defined as a **One-To-One** relationship because there can be only *one* loan record for a video at any time, and a loan record applies to just *one* video.

The final view of the links between the tables in the Relationships window should look like the one shown below in Figure 23.5.

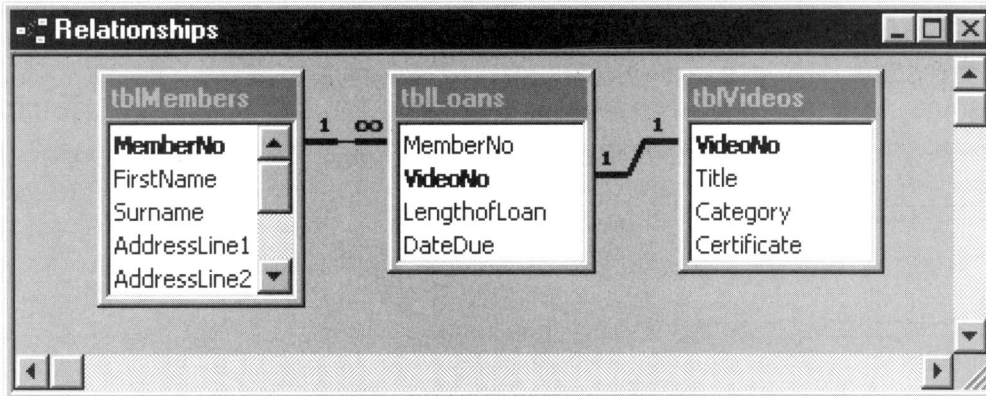

Figure 23.5: Relationships between the Members, Videos and Loans tables

- Click the **X** in the top right-hand corner of the Relationships window to **Close** and **Save** the links between the tables.

Chapter 24

Entering data in tables

This chapter describes how to enter data into a table using **Datasheet View**. You are going to enter some data into each of the tables created for the MovieZone system. This is so that there is enough data in the database to work with as we develop it further.

Task 24.1

Entering data in the Videos table

- Open the Videos table by clicking once on **Tables** in the Objects bar of the Database window and double-clicking on the icon for **tblVideos**.

    You will now see the Videos table displayed in **Datasheet View**.

- Type in the data shown in Figure 24.1 below.

VideoNo	Title	Category	Certificate
100	Vertical Limit	Act	12
101	Me, Myself and Irene	Com	15
102	Road Trip	Com	15
103	Gone In 60 seconds	Act	15
104	Close Encounters Of The Third Kind	Scf	PG
105	Pitch Black	Scf	15
106	Stuart Little	Com	U
107	Bounce	Rom	12
108	Traffic	Thr	18
109	The Way Of The Gun	Thr	18
110	The Art Of War	Act	18
111	Flawless	Com	15
112	Crouching Tiger, Hidden Dragon	Act	12
113	Unbreakable	Thr	12
114	Meet The Parents	Com	12
115	Red Planet	Scf	15
116	House	Hor	18
117	Lost In Space	Scf	PG
118	Blade	Hor	18
119	The 6th Day	Scf	15

Figure 24.1: Data to add to the Videos table

- Click the **X** in the top right-hand corner of the Videos table window. This will close the table and save the changes you've just made.

Next we'll add some data to the Members table.

Task 24.2

Entering data in the Members table

- Open the Members table by clicking once on **Tables** in the Objects bar of the Database window and double-clicking on the icon for **tblMembers**.

You will now see the Members table displayed in **Datasheet View**.

- Type in the data shown in Figure 24.2 below.

MemberNo	FirstName	Surname	AddressLine1	AddressLine2	Town	County	Postcode	DateOfBirth
100	David	Cook	41 Ashford Street	Butt Lane	Stoke-on-Trent	Staffordshire	ST7 7BZ	17/04/81
101	Heather	Porter	12 Hilltop Road	Talke	Stoke-on-Trent	Staffordshire	ST8 8NQ	28/11/87
102	Mark	Baines	29 Raleigh Drive	Tunstall	Stoke-on-Trent	Staffordshire	ST5 6SJ	05/06/82
103	Joyce	Marshall	81 Peel Street	Thornfield	Alsager	Cheshire	CH12 9TP	24/03/79
104	Anne	Harrison	71 Woodside	Brookfield	Alsager	Cheshire	CH12 8KL	19/12/82
105	Julie	Pickin	5 Holby Way	Lane Edge	Congleton	Cheshire	CH10 1XU	02/07/81
106	Nicholas	McKenna	27 Sun Street	Butt Lane	Scholar Green	Cheshire	CH9 2RJ	22/09/78
107	Harry	Johnson	59 Granger Street	Talke	Stoke-on-Trent	Staffordshire	ST8 9NP	13/04/80
108	Simon	Shelley	9 Leighton Road	Talke	Stoke-on-Trent	Staffordshire	ST8 9TC	16/10/77
109	Robert	Compton	19 Riverway	Brookfield	Alsager	Cheshire	CH12 8YB	07/08/71

Figure 24.2: Data to add to the Members table

- Click on the **X** in the top right-hand corner of the Members table window. This will close the table and save the changes you've just made.

Finally, we'll add some data to the Loans table.

Task 24.3

Entering data in the Loans table

- Open the Loans table by clicking once on **Tables** in the Objects bar of the Database window and double-clicking on the icon for **tblLoans**.

- Type in the data shown in Figure 24.3. You might think these dates seem a little strange. They've been chosen so that the same videos will always be overdue regardless of the date that you actually carry out this task.

MemberNo	VideoNo	LengthofLoan	DateDue
107	101	2	04/06/01
106	104	1	03/06/05
109	106	3	05/06/00
102	107	2	04/06/05

Figure 24.3: Data to add to the Loans table

- Click the **X** in the top right-hand corner of the Loans table window. This will close the table and save the changes you've just made.

Chapter 25

Creating and customising data entry forms

This chapter describes how to use the **Form Wizard** to create and customise **data entry forms**. These provide an efficient and user-friendly way of entering data in database tables. The new MovieZone system needs forms for the Members, Videos and Loans tables. We'll look at how to create a form for the Members table first.

Task 25.1

Creating a data entry form for the Members table

- Click once on the **Forms** tab in the Database window.
- Double-click on the **Create form by using wizard** icon.

The Form Wizard window will open (Figure 25.1).

- Click the small down-arrow on the right-hand side of the **Tables/Queries** box and choose **tblMembers** from the list.
- Put all of the fields in **tblMembers** onto the form by clicking on the right-facing double arrow >> next to the **Available Fields** box.
- Click **Next** and **Columnar**.
- Click **Next** and **Standard**.
- Click **Next** and enter *frmMembers* as the title for the form.
- Click **Finish** and the new form will appear. It should look like the one shown in Figure 25.2.

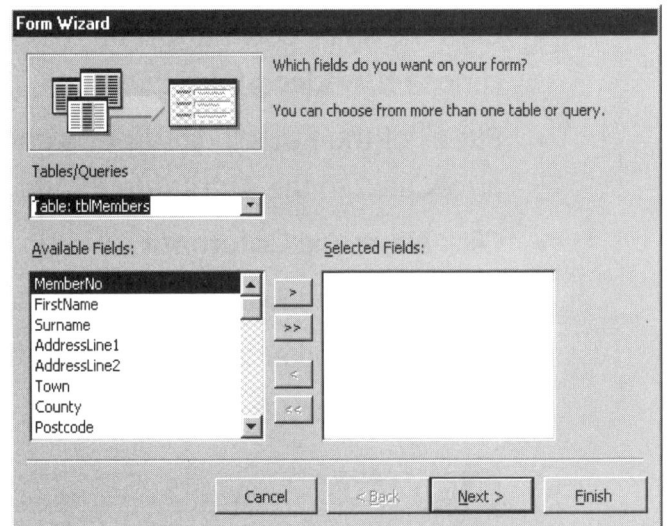

Figure 25.1: Creating the Members form

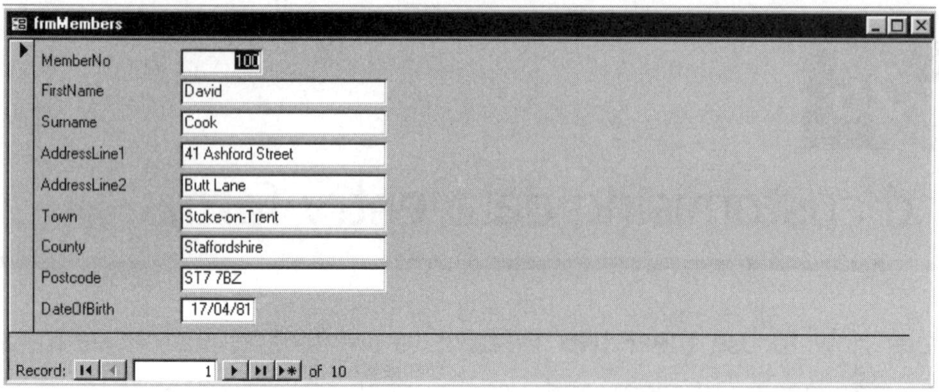

Figure 25.2: The new Members form

Next we'll create a form for the Videos table in exactly the same way.

Task 25.2

Creating a data entry form for the Videos table

- Click once on the **Forms** tab in the Database window.

- Double-click on the **Create form by using wizard** icon.

The Form Wizard window will open.

- Click the small down-arrow on the right-hand side of the **Tables/Queries** box and choose **tblVideos** from the list.

- Put all of the fields in **tblVideos** onto the form by clicking on the right-facing double arrow next to the **Available Fields** box.

- Click **Next** and **Columnar**.

- Click **Next** and **Standard**.

- Click **Next** and enter *frmVideos* as the title for the form.

- Click **Finish** and the new form will appear as shown in Figure 25.3 below.

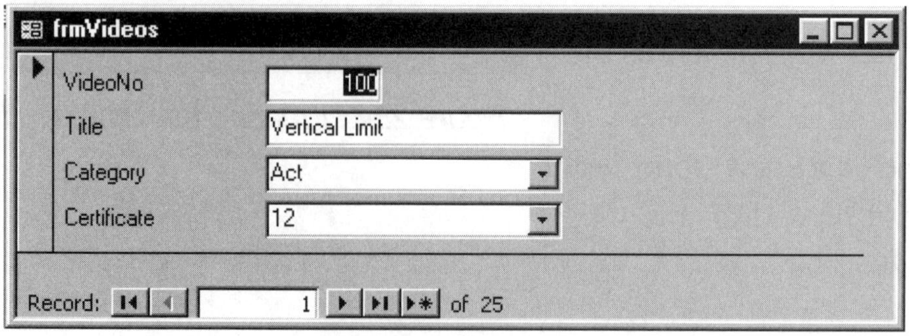

Figure 25.3: The new Videos form

Next we'll create a data entry form for loans.

Task 25.3

Creating a data entry form for the Loans table

- Click once on the **Forms** tab in the Database window.

- Double-click on the **Create form by using wizard** icon.

- The Form Wizard window will open.

- Click the small down-arrow on the right of the **Tables/Queries** box and click on **tblMembers** in the list.

- Move every field <u>except</u> **MemberNo** and **DateOfBirth** across to the **Selected Fields** box by clicking on the field name in the **Available Fields** box and the right-facing single arrow ⟩ next to it (Figure 25.4).

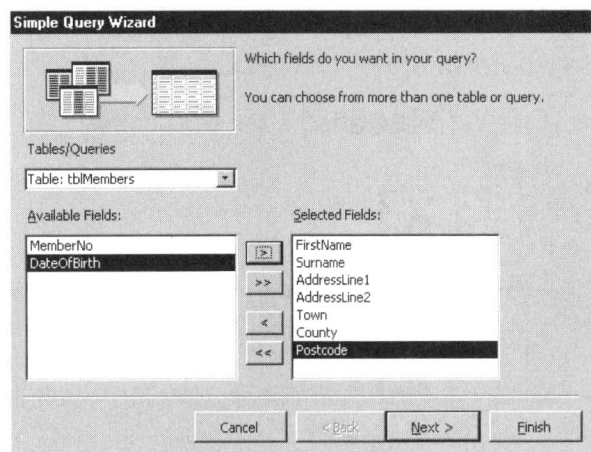

Figure 25.4: Selecting member fields

- Click the small down-arrow on the right of the **Tables/Queries** box and choose **tblLoans** from the list.

- Move the **VideoNo**, **LengthofLoan** and **DateDue** fields across to the **Selected Fields** box (Figure 25.5) as described above.

- Click **Next**.

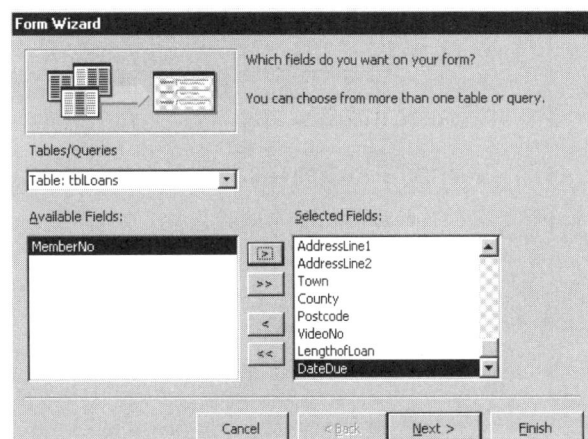

Figure 25.5: Selecting loans fields

- The next dialogue box will ask how you want to view your data. Choose **by tblMembers** and **Form with subform(s)** if they are not already selected as shown opposite in Figure 25.6.

- Click **Next**.

- Choose **Tabular** layout for your subform and click **Next**.

- Choose **Standard** style and click **Next**.

- Click **Next**.

  Enter *frmLoans* as the title for the form.

  Enter *frmLoansSubform* as the title for the subform.

- Click on **Finish** and the new form will appear. It should look something like the one shown in Figure 25.7 below.

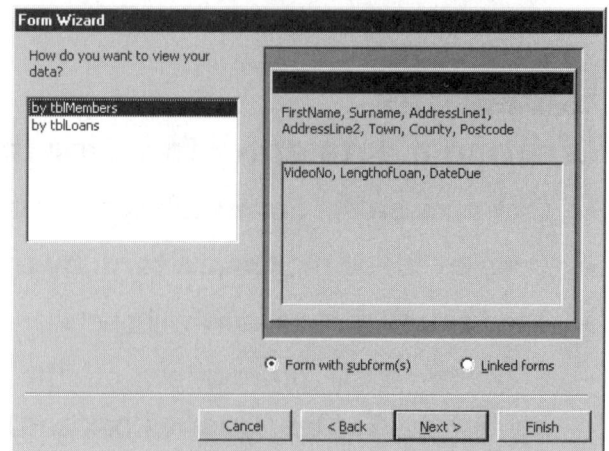

Figure 25.6: Choosing subform view

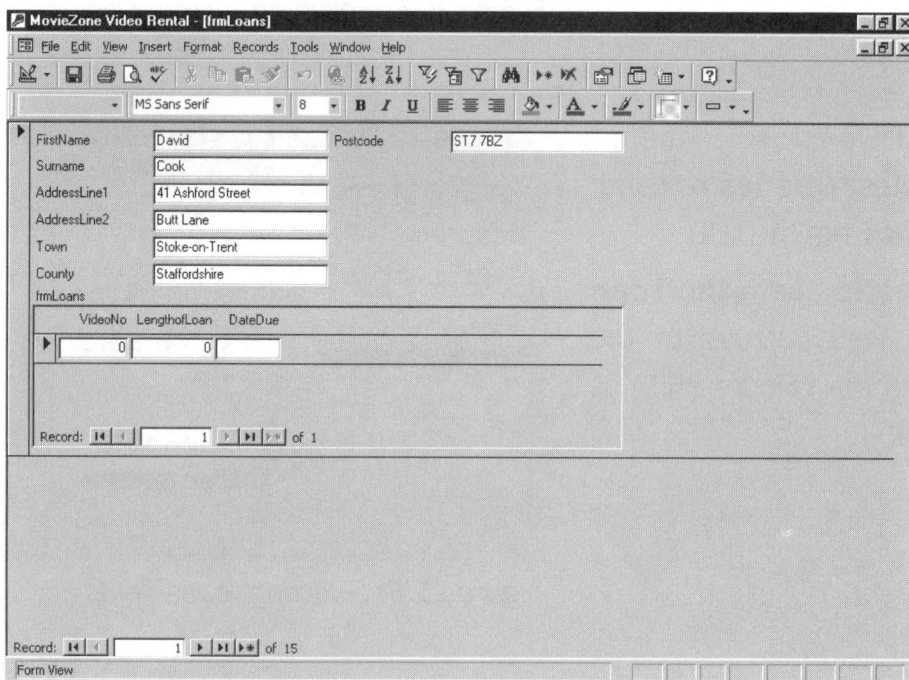

Figure 25.7: The new Loans form

Task 25.4

Customising the Members data entry form

This task describes how to customise the Members data entry form so that it matches the design on page 76 in Chapter 16.

- Start in the Database window and click on the **Forms** tab.
- Click once on the **frmMembers** icon.
- Click on the **Design View** button.

The Members form will be displayed in Design View.

- If the form doesn't fill the screen, click on the **Maximize** button in its top right-hand corner.

Now we need to make the **Detail** area of the form larger to give us enough space to work in.

- Rest the mouse pointer on the bottom right-hand corner of the detail section until it changes into this shape
- Click and hold down the left mouse button.
- Drag down and across the screen to the right (Figure 25.8) until the **Detail** section fills most of the screen as shown in Figure 25.9.

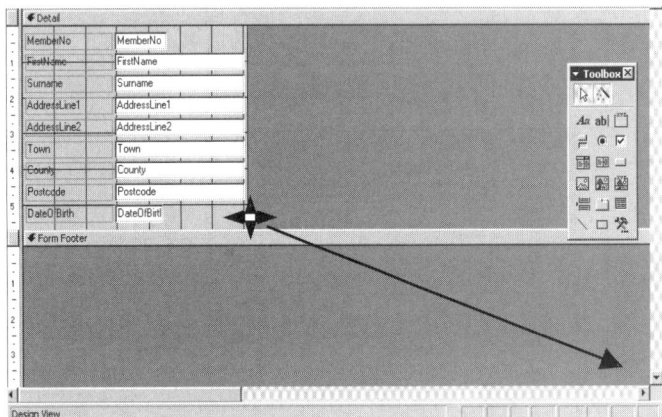

Figure 25.8: Resizing the Members form

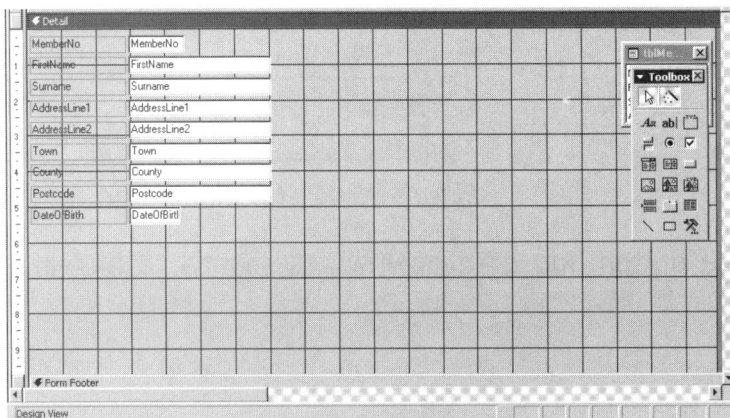

Figure 25.9: The resized Members form

Next we will tidy up the form by getting rid of some lines that won't be needed.

- Click on **View** and **Properties**.

A window will appear showing the form properties (Figure 25.10).

- Click on the **Format** tab.

- Change the setting for **Record Selectors** to **No**.

- Change the setting for **Dividing Lines** to **No**.

Figure 25.10: Form properties

Now we will change the font size of the field labels and boxes.

- Click **Edit**, **Select All** and change the font to **Arial, 11 point**.

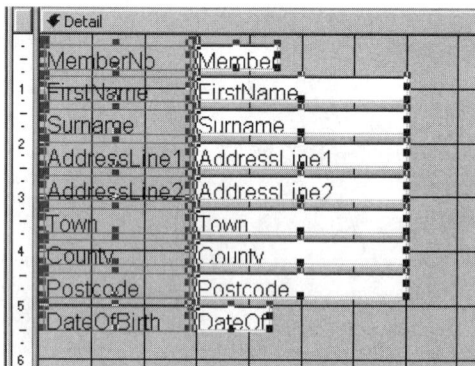

Figure 25.11: Changing font

- Rest the mouse pointer on the small black marker square at the bottom of the **DateOfBirth** field box (Figure 25.12). – it will change into this shape. ↕

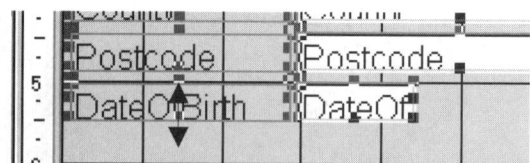

Figure 25.12: Changing size

- Click and hold the left mouse button and drag downwards slightly to increase the size of the field boxes.

- To make the field labels and boxes easier to work with we need to move them all down towards the middle of the form. To do this rest the mouse pointer in the middle of the selected field labels and boxes until you see a hand shape. Click and hold down the left mouse button and drag down and across to the right. Let go of the mouse button when the field labels and boxes are roughly in the same position as those shown in Figure 25.13 below.

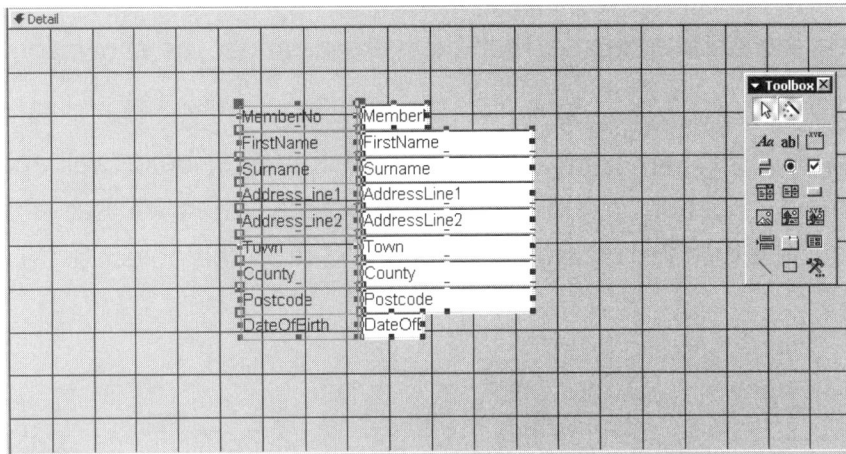

Figure 25.13: Moving groups of field labels and boxes

- Click on any blank area of the form to deselect everything.

Next we will change the text inside some of the field labels to make them easier to read and match up with the form design.

- Click inside the **MemberNo** field label and change the text to *Member Number*.

- Hold the **Shift** ⬆ key and click on each field name label in turn until they are all selected.

- Rest the mouse pointer over the small black marker on the left-hand side of the **Member Number** field label (Figure 25.14).

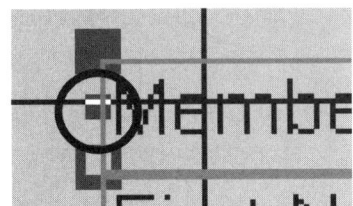

Figure 25.14

- When you see this shape ◆▶ click and hold down the left mouse button.

- Drag to the left and increase the size of the field labels until all the text in the **Member Number** field label can be seen (Figure 25.15).

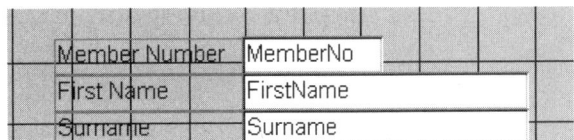

Figure 25.15

- Click inside the **FirstName** field label and insert a space between the words so that it reads *First Name*.

- Click inside the **AddressLine1** field label and insert spaces between the words so that it reads *Address Line 1*.

- Click inside the **AddressLine2** field label and insert spaces between the words so that it reads *Address Line 2*.

Next we must reposition the field boxes so that they are arranged as shown on the design for this form.

- To move an object on a form click it once and small black marker boxes will appear around it. Rest the mouse pointer on the edge of the object. When you see a hand shape, click and hold the left mouse button and drag and drop the object to its new location (Figure 25.16).

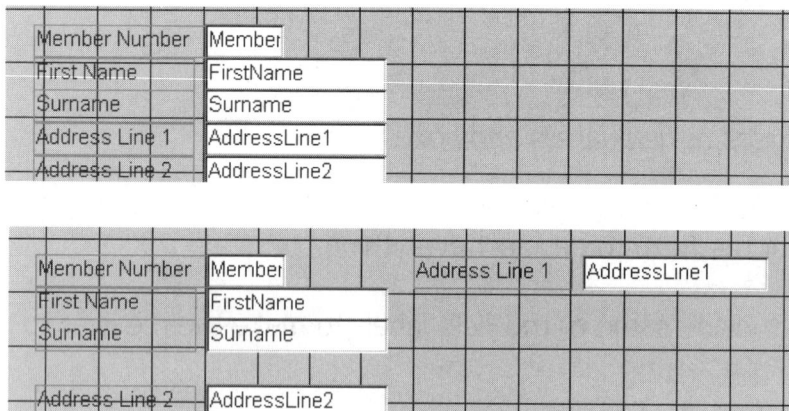

Figure 25.16: Moving objects on a form

Now we will make the labels on the field boxes bold so that they stand out on the form.

- Hold the **Shift ⬆** key and click on each field name label in turn until they are all selected.

- Click the **bold** text button **B** on the Formatting toolbar at the top of the screen.

- Click on any blank area of the form to deselect the fields.

The Members form should look now something like the one shown in Figure 25.17.

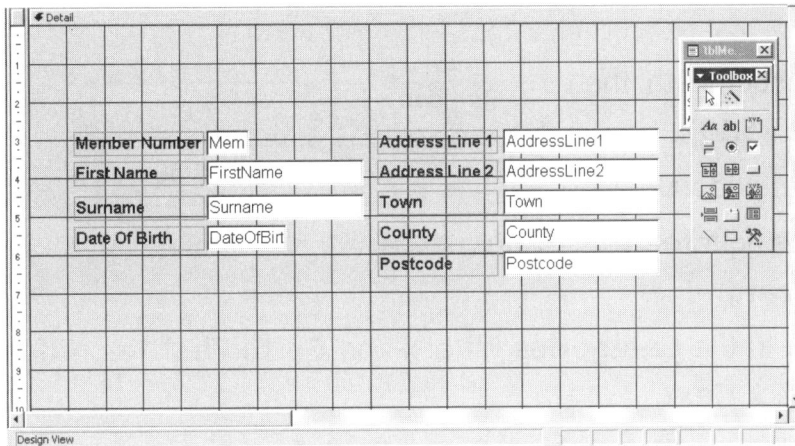

Figure 25.17: The Members form with repositioned fields

Next we will put a heading on the form.

- Click on the **Label** tool *Aa* on the toolbox.

The pointer will change to a $^+$**A** shape.

- Position the mouse pointer on the left of the form above the **MemberNo** field.

- Click and hold the left mouse button. Drag down and across to the right to open a label box.

- Type the heading *Members* (Figure 25.18).

- Click anywhere on the form away from the label box.

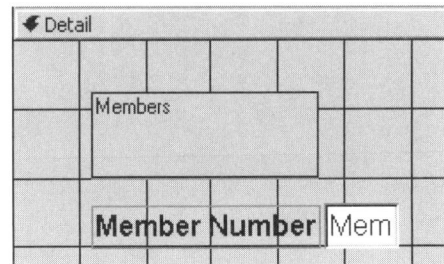

Figure 25.18: Adding a text label

Now we need to change the font type and size of the heading to match those specified in the design for this form.

- Click on the heading label box to select it.

- Change the font to **Arial**, **26 point**, **bold**.

- If necessary increase the size of the label box until all of the text is visible.

Next we need to add the command buttons shown on the form design. These will allow users to view, add and delete member details. We look at how to add a button that goes to the first record in the Members table when clicked.

- Click on the **Command Button** tool on the toolbox.

- Position the pointer just underneath the **Postcode** field box. (Figure 25.19).

- Click and hold the left mouse button.

- Drag down and across to the right to start the **Command Button Wizard**.

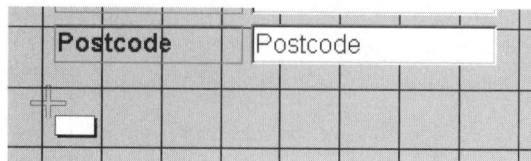

Figure 25.19

- Select **Record Navigation** in the **Categories** list box and **Go to First Record** in the **Actions** list box, then click **Next**.

- In the next dialogue box click on **Picture** and **Go to First 1** as shown in Figure 25.20 below.

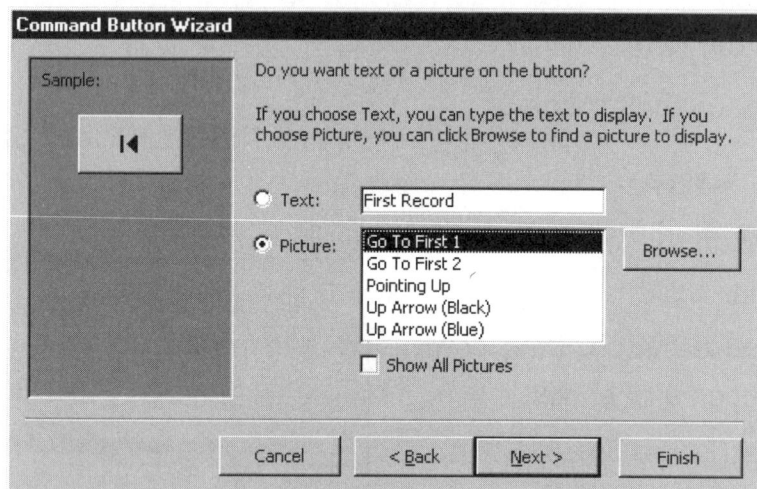

Figure 25.20: Choosing a picture for a command button

- Click **Finish** and the new command button will appear on the form as shown in Figure 25.21 opposite.

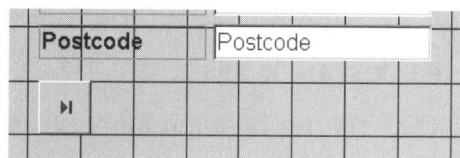

Figure 25.21

Repeat these steps to add three more command buttons that will move to the **previous**, **next** and **last records**. You should place these command buttons alongside each other. When you have finished they should look something like those shown in Figure 25.22 opposite.

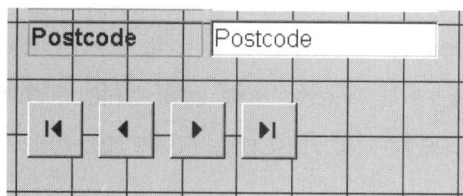

Figure 25.22

The Members form still needs two more buttons; one to create new records and another to delete existing records. We will add the command button to create new records first.

- Create a new command button next to the last record ▶️ command button.

- Select **Record Operations** in the **Categories** list box and **Add New Record** in the **Actions** list box, then click **Next**.

- In the next dialogue box click on **Picture** and **Go to New 2** if they are not already selected.

- Click **Finish** and the new command button will appear on the form.

Now we will add a command button to delete existing records.

- Create a new command button next to the new record ▶* command button.

- Select **Record Operations** in the **Categories** list box and **Delete Record** in the **Actions** list box then click **Next**.

- In the next dialogue box click on **Picture** and **Delete Record** if they are not already selected.

- Click **Finish** and the new command button will appear on the form.

You should now have a set of command buttons on the Members form like the ones shown in Figure 25.23 opposite.

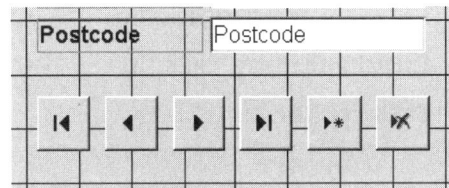

Figure 25.23

The next item we need to add to the form is a **combo box**. This will allow users to choose a member number from a drop-down list. Once the user has chosen a member number the member's details will be found and displayed on the form. The steps that must be followed to put a combo box on a form are described below.

- Click on the **Combo Box** tool 📇 on the toolbox. The mouse pointer will change to a 📇 shape.

- Position the pointer just above the **Address Line 1** field box. (Figure 25.24)

- Click and hold the left mouse button.

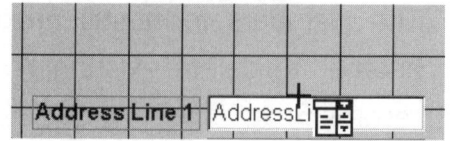

Figure 25.24

- Drag down and across to the right to create a combo box. The **Combo Box Wizard** will start up.

- In the first step of the Wizard choose **Find a record on my Form based on the value I selected in my combo box**, and click **Next** (Figure 25.25).

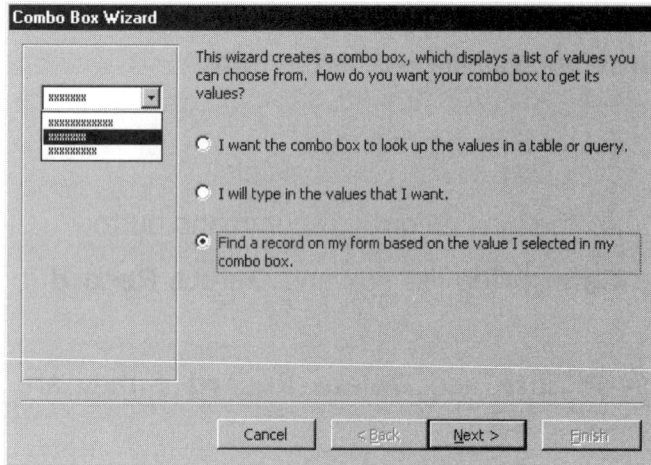

Figure 25.25: The Combo Box Wizard

- Click on **MemberNo** in the **Available Fields** box. Move it across to the **Selected Fields** box by clicking on the right-facing single arrow ⟩ (Figure 25.26) then click **Next**.

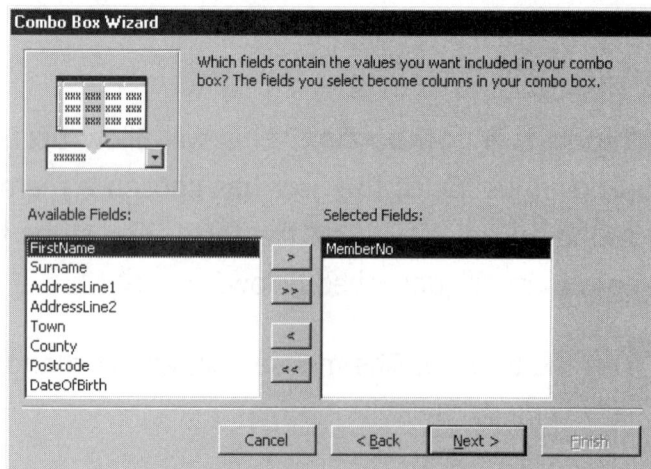

Figure 25.26: Choosing fields for a Combo Box

In the next window rest the mouse pointer on the edge of the **MemberNo** column heading. You will see it change to this shape. ←|→

- Click and hold the left mouse button. Drag across to the left until the column is just wide enough for the Member numbers (Figure 25.27).

- Click **Next**.

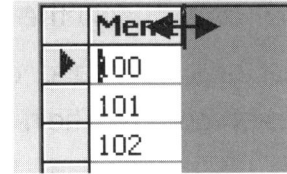

Figure 25.27

- In the next window enter *Find member with membership number* as the label for your combo box, and click **Finish**. The new combo box will appear on the form.

- Change the font to **Arial**, **11 point**, **Bold**.

- Increase the size of the combo box label until all the text is visible.

We have now made most of the changes needed to make the Members form match up with its design. It should look something like the one shown in Figure 25.28 below. The only missing item is a command button that will allow users to move from the form to the Main menu. We look at how to create the Main menu and add this button in Chapter 30.

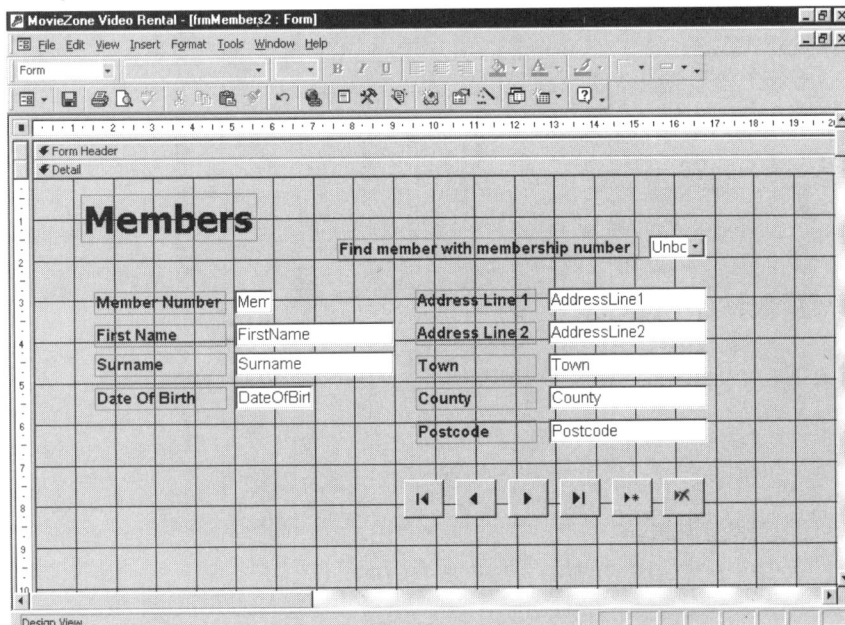

Figure 25.28: The customised Members form in Design View

- Click the **X** in the top right-hand corner of the form window to close the form.

- Click **Yes** to save changes to the design of the form.

Task 25.5

Customising the videos data entry form

This task describes how to customise the videos data entry form so that it matches the design on page 77 in Chapter 16. Most of the steps are similar to those described in the last task so a little less detail is given this time.

- Start in the Database window and click on the **Forms** tab.

- Click once on the **frmVideos** icon.

- Click on the **Design View** button.

The Videos form will be displayed in Design View.

- If the form doesn't fill the screen click on the **Maximize** button in its top right-hand corner.

- Make the **Detail** area of the form larger until it fills most of the screen as shown in Figure 25.29 below.

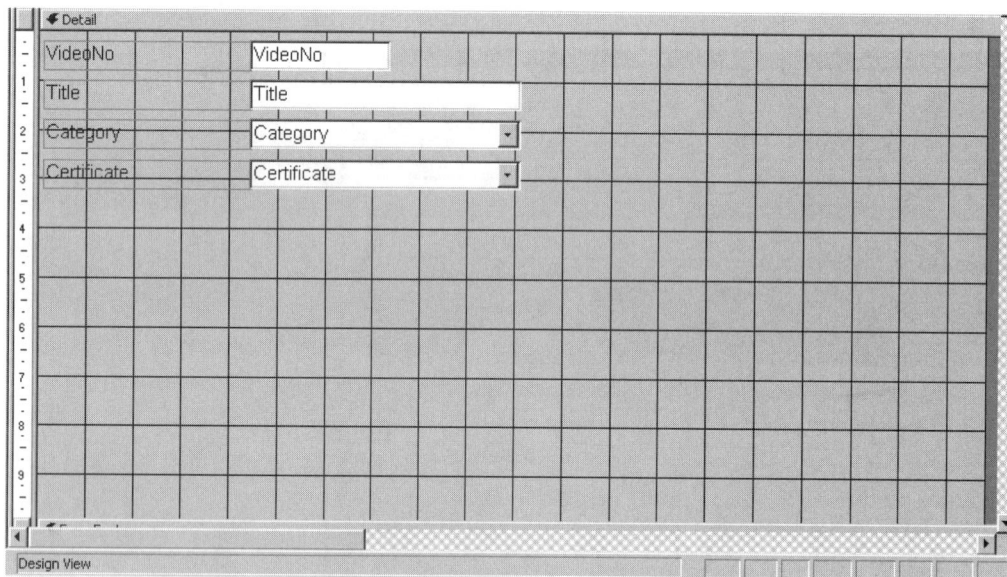

Figure 25.29: The resized Detail section of the Videos form

Next, tidy up the form by getting rid of the lines that aren't needed.

- Click on **View** and **Properties**.

- In the Form window click on the **Format** tab in the Form Properties window.

- Change the setting for **Record Selectors** to **No**.

- Change the setting for **Dividing Lines** to **No**.

Now change the font size of the field labels and boxes.

- Click **Edit**, **Select All** and change the font to **Arial, 11 point**.
- If necessary increase the size of the field boxes.
- Click on any blank area of the form to deselect everything.

Next we will change the text of the **VideoNo** field label to make it easier to read and match up with the form design.

- Click inside the **VideoNo** field label and change the text to *Video Number*.
- Hold the **Shift** ⬆ key and click on each field name label in turn until they are all selected.
- Rest the mouse pointer over the small black marker on the left-hand side of the **Video Number** field label (Figure 25.30).

Figure 25.30

- When you see this shape ◄► click and hold down the left mouse button.
- Drag to the left and increase the size of the field labels until all the text in the **Video Number** field label can be seen.

Now we will make the text in the field name labels bold so that they stand out on the form.

- Hold the **Shift** ⬆ key and click on each field name label in turn until they are all selected.
- Click the **Bold** button **B** on the Formatting toolbar at the top of the screen.
- Click on any blank area of the form to deselect the fields.

Next, reposition the field boxes so that they are arranged as shown on the design for this form. When you have finished, the Videos form should look something like the one shown in Figure 25.31.

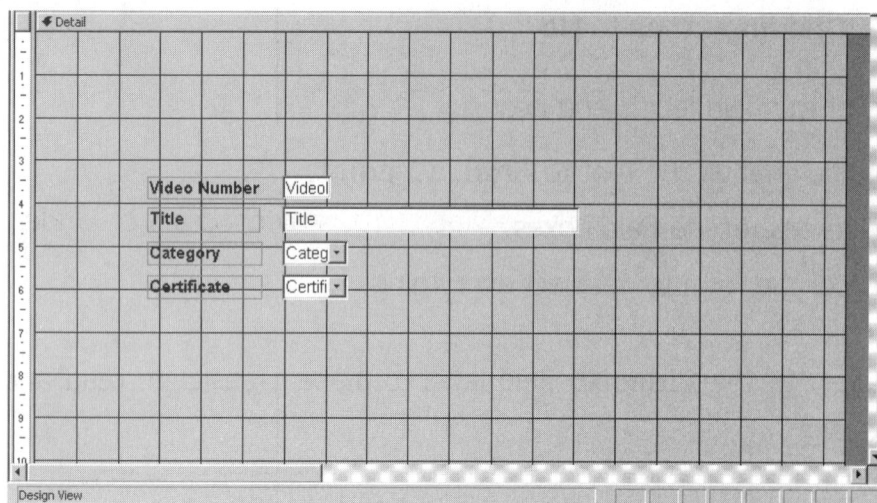

Figure 25.31: The Videos form with fields repositioned

Next we will put a heading on the form.

- Click on the **Label** tool *Aa* on the toolbox.
- Position the ^{+}A pointer above the **VideoNo** field.
- Open up a label box and type the heading *Videos*.
- Click anywhere on the form away from the label box.
- Change the font type and size for the heading to **Arial**, **26 point**, **bold**.
- If necessary increase the size of the text label box until all of the text is visible.

Now we will add the command buttons shown on the form design. To do this you need to repeat the steps described in Task 25.4 on pages 131-133.

- First add four command buttons that will move to the **first**, **previous**, **next** and **last records**. Place these command buttons alongside each other to the right of the **Certificate** field box as shown in Figure 25.32 below.

Figure 25.32

- Next add two more command buttons to **add** and **delete** records. Place these command buttons next to the ones you have just created as shown in Figure 25.33.

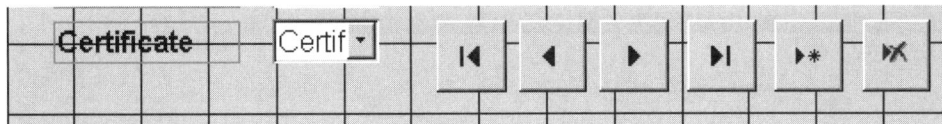

Figure 25.33

Now add a **combo box** that will allow users to view video details by choosing the video number from a drop-down list.

- Click on the **Combo Box** tool on the toolbox.

- Create a combo box on the right-hand side of the form in between the *Videos* heading and the **VideoNo** field box. (Figure 25.34).

Figure 25.34

- In the first step of the **Combo Box Wizard** choose **Find a record on my Form based on the value I selected in my combo box**, and click **Next**.

- Click on **VideoNo** in the **Available Fields** box. Move it across to the **Selected Fields** box by clicking on the right-facing single arrow and click **Next**.

- In the next window change the size of the **VideoNo** column until it is just wide enough for the video numbers and click **Next**.

- In the next window enter *Find video with video number* as the label for the combo box, and click **Finish**. The new combo box will appear on the form.

- Change the font to **Arial**, **11 point** and **Bold**.

- Increase the size of the combo box label until all of the text is visible.

We have now made most of the changes needed to make the Videos form match up with its design. It should look something like the one shown in Figure 25.35. The only missing items are two command buttons that will allow users to move from the form to the Find Videos menu or the Main menu. We look at how to add these buttons in Chapter 30.

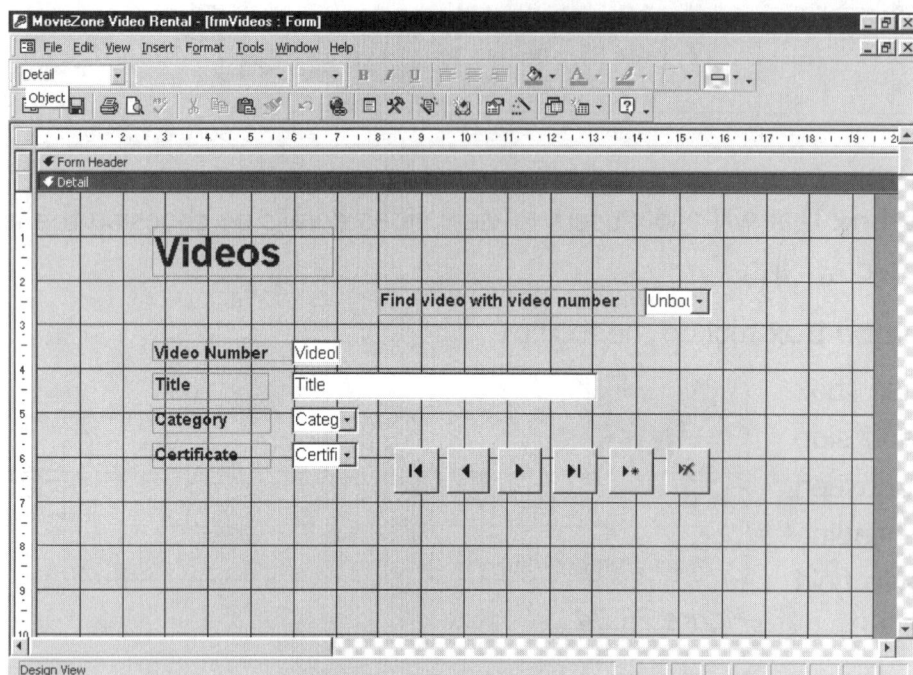

Figure 25.35: The customised Videos form in Design View

- Click the **X** in the top right-hand corner of the form window to close the form.

- Click **Yes** to save changes to the design of the form.

Task 25.6

Customising the loans data entry form

This task describes how to customise the Loans data entry form so that it matches the design on page 78 in Chapter 16. Most of the steps are similar to those described in the last two tasks so a little less detail is given this time around. This form is best dealt with in two stages. First of all we will look at how to customise the main part of the form, where member details are displayed. Then we will go on to customise the subform where loan details for a member are displayed.

- Start in the Database window and click on the **Forms** tab.

- Click once on the **frmLoans** icon.

- Click on the **Design View** button.

The Loans form will be displayed in Design View.

- If the form doesn't fill the screen click on the **Maximize** button ☐ in its top right-hand corner.

- Make the **Detail** area of the form larger until it fills most of the screen as shown in Figure 25.36 below.

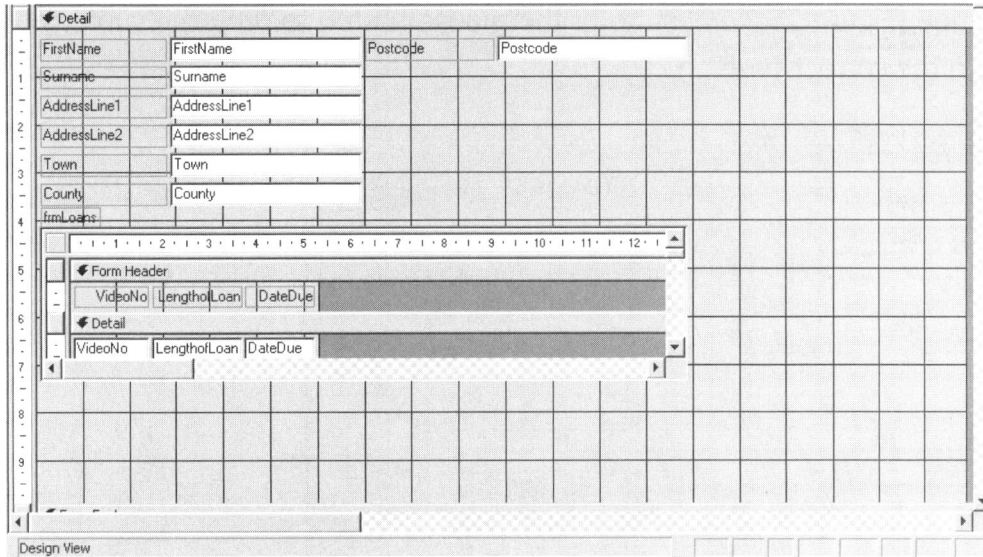

Figure 25.36: The resized Detail section of the Loans form

Next, tidy up the form by getting rid of some lines that aren't needed.

- Click on **View** and **Properties**.

- In the form window click on the **Format** tab in the Form Properties window.

- Change the setting for **Record Selectors** to **No**.

- Change the setting for **Navigation Buttons** to **No**.

- Change the setting for **Dividing Lines** to **No**.

Now change the font size of the field labels and boxes.

- Click **Edit**, **Select All** and change the font to **Arial, 11 point**.

- Add spaces between the words in the **FirstName**, **AddressLine1** and **AddressLine2** field labels so that they can be read more easily.

- Click on any blank area of the form to deselect everything.

To make the form easier to work with we need to move the field labels, boxes and subform. We will move the subform first.

- Click on the subform.

- Rest the pointer on the edge of the subform until it changes to a hand shape.

- Click and hold the left mouse button.

- Drag the subform down and across to the right towards the bottom centre of the **Detail** section (Figure 25.37). Let go of the mouse button to drop the subform when it is in the correct position.

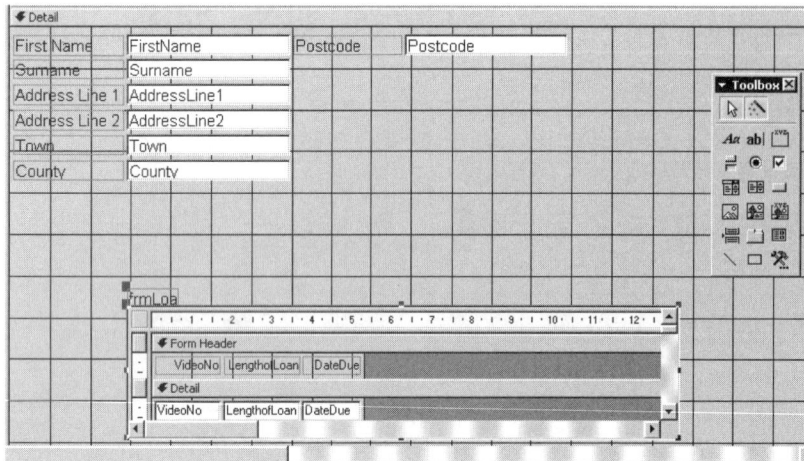

Figure 25.37: The repositioned loans subform

Now we will move the Member field labels and boxes.

- Hold the **Shift** ⬆ key and click on each field name label and box in turn until they are all selected (Figure 25.38).

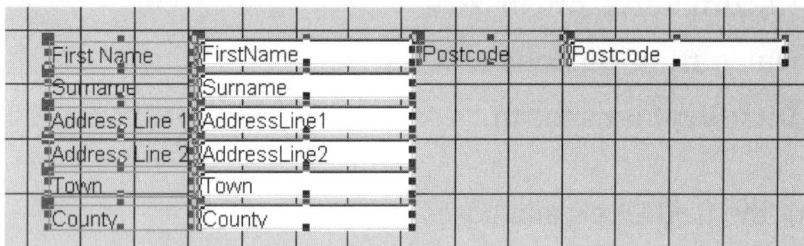

Figure 25.38: Member field name labels and boxes selected

- Rest the mouse pointer in the middle of the selected field labels and boxes until you see a hand shape.

- Click and hold down the left mouse button and drag down and across to the right. Let go of the mouse button when the field labels and boxes are roughly in the same position as those shown in Figure 25.39.

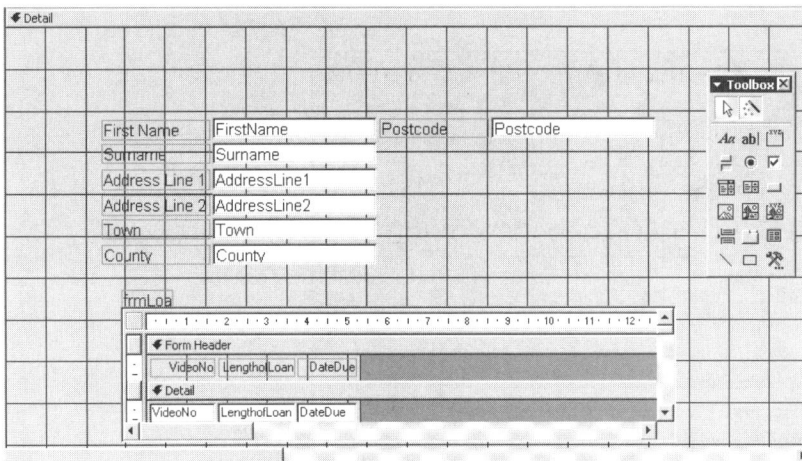

Figure 25.39: Member field name labels and boxes selected

Now make the field labels bold so that they stand out on the form.

- Hold the **Shift ⬆** key and click on each field label in turn until they are all selected (Figure 25.40).

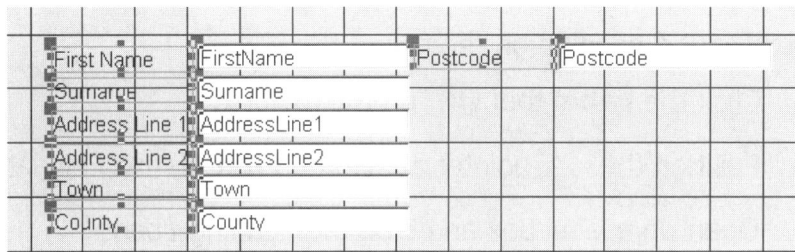

Figure 25.40: Member field name labels selected

- Click the **Bold** button **B** on the Formatting toolbar at the top of the screen.

- Rest the mouse pointer over the small black marker on the left-hand side of the **First Name** field label (Figure 25.41).

Figure 25.41

- When you see this shape ⬌ click and hold down the left mouse button.

- Drag to the left to increase the size of the field labels until all the text is visible.

- Click on any blank area of the form to deselect the fields.

Now reposition the member field labels and boxes so that they are arranged as shown on the design for this form. When you have finished, the Loans form should look something like the one shown in Figure 25.42.

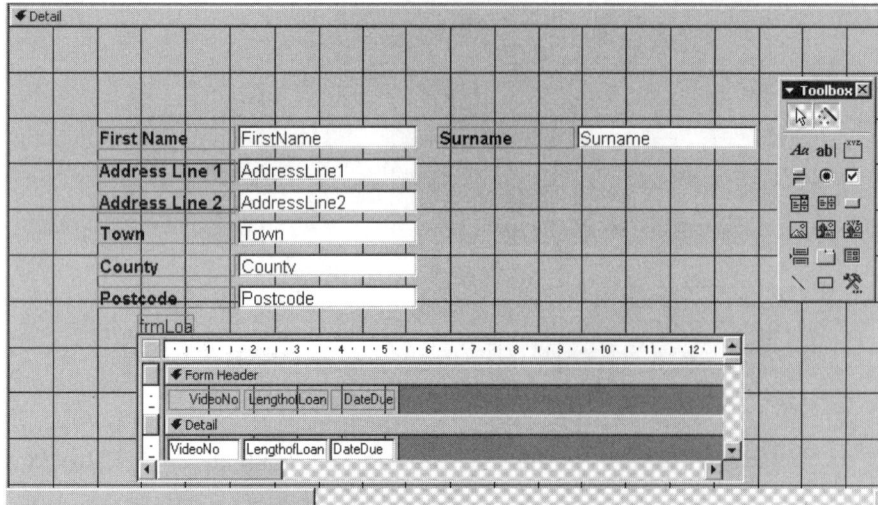

Figure 25.42: The Loans form with objects repositioned

Next, put a heading on the form.

- Click the **Label** tool *Aa* on the toolbox.

- Position the ^+A pointer above the **First Name** field label.

- Open up a label box and type the heading *Loans*.

- Click anywhere on the form away from the label box.

- Change the font type and size for the heading to **Arial**, **26 point**, **bold**.

- If necessary increase the size of the label box until all of the text is visible.

Now add the command buttons shown on the form design.

- Add four command buttons that will move to the **first**, **previous**, **next** and **last records**. Place these command buttons alongside each other underneath the **Surname** field box as shown in Figure 25.43 opposite.

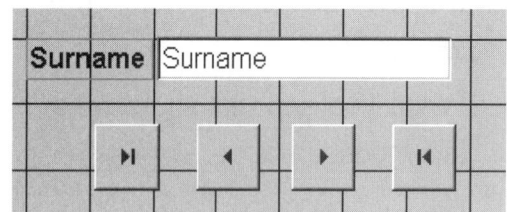

Figure 25.43

Now add a **combo box** that will allow users to view the loan details for a member by choosing the member number from a drop-down list.

- Click on the **Combo Box** tool on the toolbox.

- Create the combo box on the right-hand side of the form in between the **Loans** heading and the **Surname** field box. (Figure 25.44)

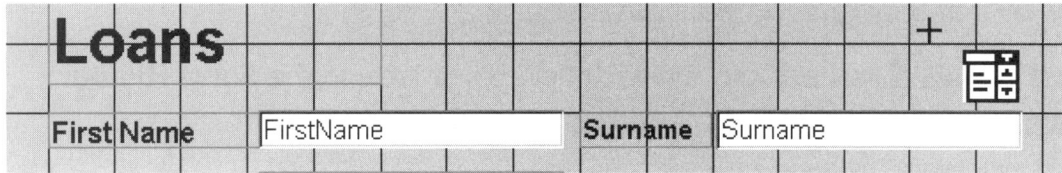

Figure 25.44

- In the first step of the **Combo Box Wizard** choose **Find a record on my Form based on the value I selected in my combo box**, and click **Next**.

- Click on **MemberNo** in the **Available Fields** box. Move it across to the **Selected Fields** box by clicking on the right-facing single arrow $\boxed{>}$ and click **Next**.

- In the next window change the size of the **MemberNo** column until it is just wide enough for the loan numbers and click **Next**.

- In the next window enter *Find loan details for member number* as the label for the combo box, and click **Finish**. The new combo box will appear on the form.

- Change the font to **Arial**, **11 point** and **Bold**.

- Increase the size of the combo box label until all of the text is visible.

Now we will deal with the appearance of the subform.

- Click on the label at the top of the subform. (Figure 25.45)

- Click on the **Cut** ✂ button on the Formatting toolbar to remove the label.

Figure 25.45

- Click anywhere in the subform.

- Rest the mouse pointer on the edge of the working area of the subform until you see this shape ◀┼▶

- Click and hold down the left mouse button and drag to the right until the subform looks like the one shown below in Figure 25.46.

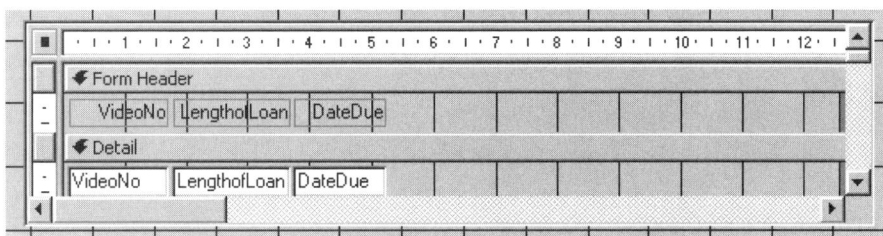

Figure 25.46

Now we will change the appearance of the field labels and boxes on the subform.

- Add spaces between the words in the **VideoNo**, **LengthofLoan** and **DateDue** field labels so that they can be read more easily.

- Hold the **Shift** ⬆ key and click on each field name label in the **Form Header** section.

- Change the font to **Arial, 11 point**, **bold**.

- Click **Align Left** ≣ on the Formatting toolbar at the top of the screen.

- Increase the size of each field label so that all of the text is visible – you will need to space the labels out as you do this by dragging and dropping.

- Click on any blank area of the subform to deselect the field labels.

- Hold the **Shift** ⬆ key and click on each field box in the **Form Header** in the **Detail** section.

- Change the font to **Arial, 11 point**, **bold**.

- Click **Align Left** ≣ on the Formatting toolbar at the top of the screen.

- Drag and drop each field box in the **Detail** section so that it is lined up with the corresponding field name label in the **Form Header** section. When you have finished, the subform should look something like the one shown in Figure 25.47 below.

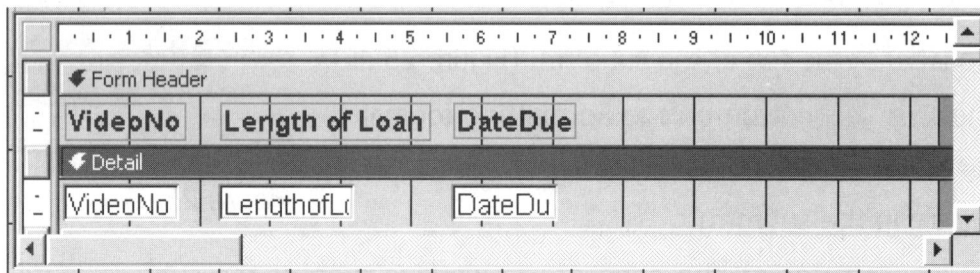

Figure 25.47: The Loans subform after changes to field labels and boxes

Put a text label next to the **LengthofLoan** field box in the **Detail** section.

- First make the **LengthofLoan** field box roughly half its original size as shown in Figure 25.48.

- Click on the **Label** tool *Aa* on the toolbox.

- Position the ⁺A pointer next to the **LengthofLoan** field box.

- Open up a label box and type *Days*.

- Click anywhere on the form away from the label box.

- Click back on the label box to reselect it.

- Change the font type and size for the label to **Arial**, **11 point**.

Figure 25.48

- Increase the size of the label box until all of the text is visible (Figure 25.48).

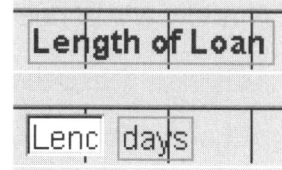

The last change that needs to be made in the **Detail** section is to make the **DateDue** field box slightly larger.

- Click on the **DateDue** field box in the **Detail** section.

- Increase the size of the field box until it is approximately the same size as the **Date Due** label in the **Form Header** section (Figure 25.49).

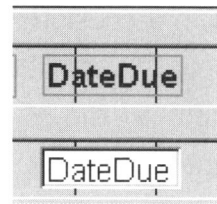

Figure 25.49

Next we need to add command buttons to **add** and **delete** loan records in the **Form Header** section. We are putting these command buttons on the subform because it is *Loan records* <u>not</u> Member records that we need to add and delete. The steps you need to follow are the same as those described in Task 25.4 on page 135. Place these command buttons next to the **Date Due** field label.

Finally we will get rid of some lines and controls that aren't needed on the subform.

- Rest the mouse pointer on the bottom edge of the subform.

- Click the mouse button and marker boxes will appear all around the subform.

- Choose **View**, **Properties** from the Menu bar.

A window will appear showing the **Subform/Subreport** properties.

- Click on the **Format** tab.

- Change the setting for **Border Style** to **Transparent**.

- Close the Properties window by clicking the **X** in the top right-hand corner.

- Rest the mouse pointer in the scroll bar at the bottom of the subform.

- Click the mouse button and a black square will appear in the top left corner of the subform.

- Choose **View**, **Properties** from the Menu bar.

A window will appear showing the **Form** properties.

- Change the setting for **Record Selectors** to **No**.
- Change the setting for **Navigation Buttons** to **No**.
- Change the setting for **Dividing Lines** to **No**.
- Close the properties window by clicking the **X** in the top right-hand corner.

We have now made most of the changes needed to make the Loans form match up with its design. It should look something like the one shown in Figure 25.50 below. The only missing items are two command buttons that will allow users to move from the form to the Main menu or print the Overdue report. We look at how to add these buttons in Chapter 30.

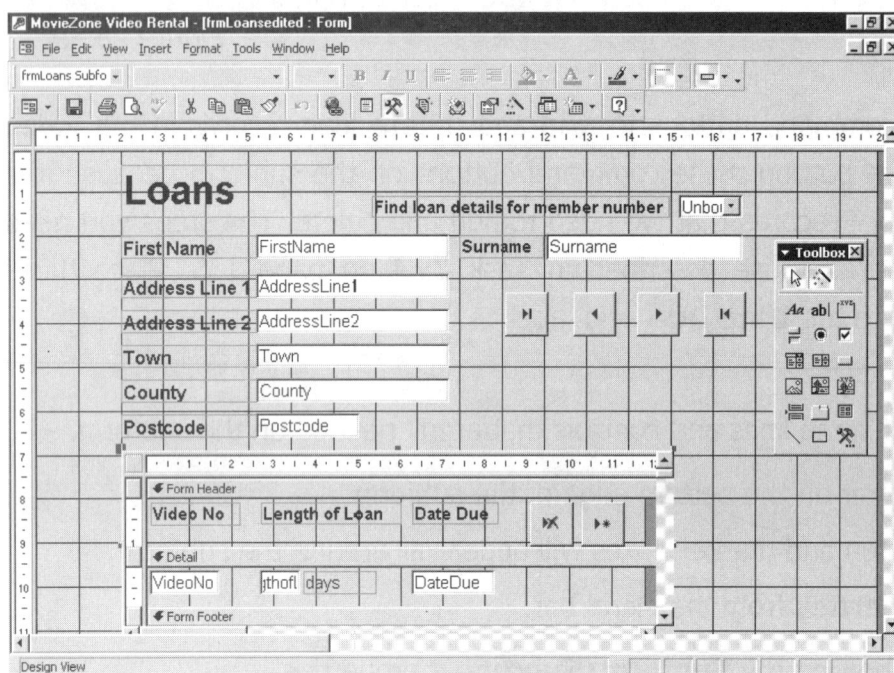

Figure 25.50: The customised Loans form in Design View

- Click the **X** in the top right-hand corner of the form window to close the form.
- Choose **Yes** to save changes to the design of the form.

Chapter 26

Using data entry forms

This chapter describes how to use the data entry forms we have created to enter data. We're going to add some more records to each table so that there's enough data in the database for testing later on.

First we'll add some more data to the Members table.

Task 26.1

Adding data to the Members table

- Click on **Forms** in the Objects bar of the Database window.
- Double-click on **frmMembers** to open the Members form.
- Click on the **New Record** command button. ▶*
- Add the data shown in Figure 26.1 below.

  You can move from one field box to another by pointing and clicking with the mouse, using the arrow keys [←→↑↓] or pressing the **Tab** key. 🔄

MemberNo	FirstName	Surname	AddressLine1	AddressLine2	Town	County	Postcode	DateOfBirth
110	Paul	Holmes	98 Salter Street	Thornfield	Alsager	Cheshire	CH12 8HW	11/02/81
111	Kaka	Singh	76 Merrick Drive	Talke	Stoke-on-Trent	Staffordshire	ST8 7BP	29/12/78
112	Hilary	Kramer	21 Dane Bank	Lane Edge	Congleton	Cheshire	CH10 2SH	14/04/83
113	Bernice	Osbourne	39 Horton Street	Talke	Stoke-on-Trent	Staffordshire	ST8 9BJ	07/09/76
114	John	Warne	8 Holby Way	Lane Edge	Congleton	Cheshire	CH10 2CK	27/05/82

Figure 26.1: More data to add to the Members table

- Close the Members form by clicking the **X** in its top right-hand corner.

Next we'll add some more data to the Videos table.

- Click on **Forms** in the Objects bar of the Database window.

- Double-click on **frmVideos** to open the Videos form.

- Click on the **New Record** command button. ▶✳

- Add the data shown in Figure 26.2 below.

	VideoNo	Title	Category	Certificate
	120	Scream 3	Hor	18
	121	Shirley Valentine	Com	PG
	122	Highlander	Scf	15
	123	Armageddon	Scf	12
	124	The Skulls	Thr	15

Figure 26.2: More data to add to the Videos table

- Close the Videos form by clicking the **X** in its top right-hand corner.

Finally we'll add some more data to the Loans table.

- Click on **Forms** in the Objects bar of the Database window.

- Double-click on **frmLoans** to open the Loans form.

- Click on the **New Record** command button. ▶✳

- Add the data shown in Figure 26.3 below.

	MemberNo	VideoNo	LengthofLoan	DateDue
	111	112	1	01/06/01
	111	102	2	02/06/01
	112	109	1	03/06/01
	114	103	2	29/05/01
	114	110	2	27/05/01

Figure 26.3: More data to add to the Loans table

- Close the Loans form by clicking the **X** in its top right-hand corner.

Chapter 27

Verification and validation

Data is only useful as long as it is correct and up-to-date. Because of this it is important to check data when it is entered to make sure that it is both sensible and correct. Failing to check data for errors before it is processed could cause the final output to be nonsense. There are two methods that are used to check data when it is input. These are called **verification** and **validation**.

Verification is checking to make sure that data has been entered correctly. Verification is often carried out by getting two users to enter the same set of data at different computers. Once both users have entered the data the two sets of data are compared to check that they match up. Any data that does not match up is rejected. Verification can also be carried out by software that might, for example, ask for the same data to be entered twice. If both entries don't match up the data is rejected.

Validation checks are carried out by software to make sure that data that has been entered is **allowable** and **sensible**. The computer rejects data that is not sensible or allowed.

In this chapter we'll look at how to use verification and validation to make sure that the data in each one of the tables in the new database is correct and sensible.

Task 27.1

Verifying the data in the new tables

We will use **visual verification** to check that the data which has been entered in the new database tables does not contain any errors. To do this we need to print out each table and look carefully at the data in each record. If there are any mistakes they need to be marked and corrected before we carry on setting up the new system.

We'll do this for the Videos table first.

- Click on **Tables** in the Objects bar of the Database window.
- Double-click on **tblVideos** to open the Videos table.
- Click on the **Print** icon in the Formatting toolbar at the top of the screen. 🖨

This will print out the Videos table. Look carefully at the data on this printout and mark any fields where there are mistakes. Do this by drawing a circle around the field, underlining it or marking it with a highlighting pen. You should end up with a printout of the table that looks something like the one shown below in Figure 27.1.

VideoNo	Title	Category	Certificate
10	Vertical Limit	Act	12
101	Me, Myself and Irene	Com	15
102	Road Trip	Com	15
103	Gone In 60 seconds	Act	15
104	Close Encounters Of The Third Kind	Scf	PG
105	Pitcj Black	Scf	15
106	Stuart Little	Com	18
107	Bounce	Rom	12
108	Traffic	Com	18
109	The Way OfThe Gun	Thr	18
110	The Art Of War	Act	18
111	Flawless	Com	15
112	Crouching Tiger, Hidden Dragon	Act	12
113	Unbreakable	Thr	12
114	Meet The Parents	Hor	18
115	Red Planet	Scf	15
116	House	Hor	U
117	Lost In Space	Scf	PG
118	Blad	Hor	18
119	The 6th Day	Scf	15
120	Scream 3	Hor	18
121	Shirley Valentine	Hor	PG
122	High lander	Scf	15
123	Armageddon	Scf	12
1124	The Skulls	Thr	15

Figure 27.1: The Videos table after visual verification with data errors marked

Tip If you don't find any mistakes put some in a few fields. This might sound strange but it's easier to prove that you've checked for mistakes if there are some that the examiner can see!

- After marking any mistakes – we'll call these **data errors** from now on – write at the bottom of this printout "**Data errors found in the video table during visual verification**". This printout proves that you've carried out verification and found the data errors which need correcting. Next we need to correct these data errors.

- Make sure the Videos table is displayed – if it isn't double-click on **tblVideos** in the Database window.

- Click with the mouse in each field that needs correcting and enter the correct data.

- Once you're sure that all of the corrections have been made click once again on the **Print** icon at the top of the screen.

- Write at the bottom of this printout "**Videos table after visual verification with data errors corrected**". This printout proves that you've corrected the data errors found during visual verification.

Now repeat this process for the Members and Loans tables.

Task 27.2

Setting up data validation checks for the Members table

The only validation rule specified in the Members table design is that values in the **MemberNo** field must be between 1 and 5000. To set up this validation check follow the steps listed below.

- Start in the Database window and click on the **Tables** object type.

- Click on the **tblMembers** icon.

- Click on the **Design** icon   📐 Design   to open the table in Design View.

- The **MemberNo** field should already be highlighted – if it isn't, click next to **MemberNo** in the **Field Name** column.

- Click in the **Validation Rule** box and type *Between 1 And 5000* (Figure 27.2). This sets the rule that Access 2000 will use to check data entered in this field.

- Click in the **Validation Text** box and type *Enter a number between 1 and 5000* (Figure 27.2). This specifies the message that Access 2000 must display if data that breaks the validation rule is entered in this field.

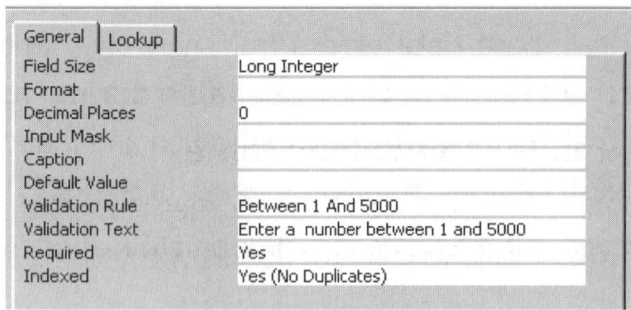

Field Size	Long Integer
Format	
Decimal Places	0
Input Mask	
Caption	
Default Value	
Validation Rule	Between 1 And 5000
Validation Text	Enter a number between 1 and 5000
Required	Yes
Indexed	Yes (No Duplicates)

Figure 27.2: The validation rule for MemberNo

- Click on the **View** icon ⬚ in the toolbar.

- Click on **Yes** to save the table.

The Members table will be displayed. We are now ready to test the new validation rule.

- Click in the **MemberNo** field for the first member, delete the current value and enter *5002*. The new validation rule should check this data and reject it as shown in Figure 27.3 opposite.

Figure 27.3: Testing the validation rule for MemberNo

- Click on **OK** and change the **MemberNo** for the first member back to *100*.

- Close the Members table by clicking the **X** in the top right-hand corner of its window.

Note that Access automatically checks that anything you enter in a field defined with a field type of **Date/Time** is a valid date. That's why it is important to use this field type for dates, rather than just using the default **Text** data type.

You have now set up the validation checks specified in the Members table design.

Task 27.3

Setting up data validation checks for the Videos table

The first validation rule specified in the Videos table design is that values in the VideoNo field must be between 1 and 1000. To set up this validation rule follow the steps listed below.

- Start in the Database window and click on the **Tables** object type.

- Click on the **tblVideos** icon.

- Click on the **Design** icon ▦ Design to open the table in Design View.

- The **VideoNo** field should already be highlighted – if it isn't, click next to **VideoNo** in the **Field Name** column.

- Click in the **Validation Rule** box and type *Between 1 And 1000* (Figure 27.4).

- Click in the **Validation Text** box and type *Enter a number between 1 and 1000* (Figure 27.4).

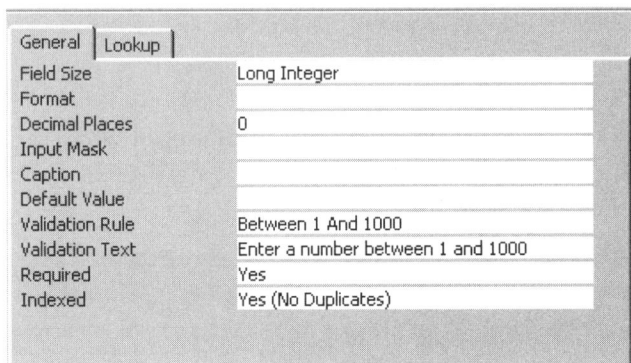

General	Lookup
Field Size	Long Integer
Format	
Decimal Places	0
Input Mask	
Caption	
Default Value	
Validation Rule	Between 1 And 1000
Validation Text	Enter a number between 1 and 1000
Required	Yes
Indexed	Yes (No Duplicates)

Figure 27.4: The validation rule for VideoNo

- Click on the **View** icon ▦ in the toolbar.

- Click on **Yes** to save the table.

The Videos table will be displayed. We are now ready to test the new validation rule.

- Click in the **VideoNo** field for the first video, delete the current value and enter *1001.* The new validation rule should check this data and reject it as shown in Figure 27.5.

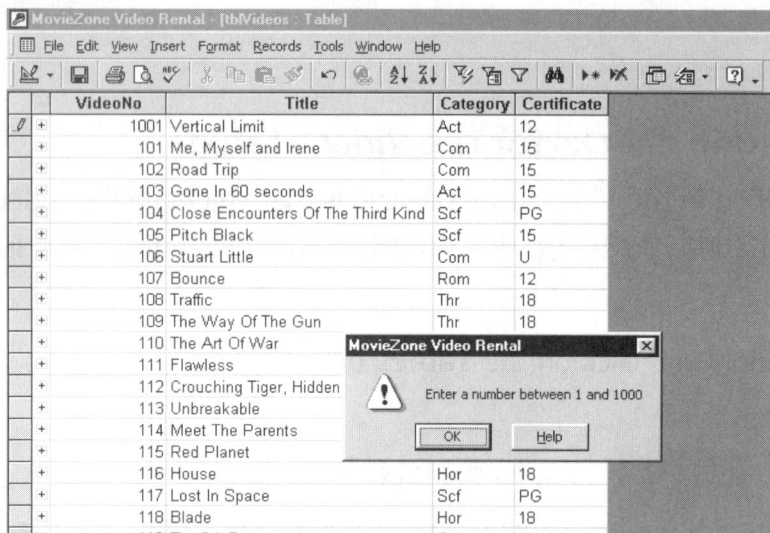

Figure 27.5: Testing the validation rule for VideoNo

- Click on **OK** and change the **VideoNo** for the first video back to *100*.

The next validation rule specified in the Videos table design is that the **Category** field can only contain one of the values *Act*, *Com*, *Hor*, *Scf* or *Thr*. To set up this validation rule follow the steps listed below.

- Click on the **Design** icon [Design] to open the Videos table in Design View.
- Click next to **Category** in the **Field Name** column.
- Click in the **Validation Rule** box and type *"Act" Or "Com" Or "Hor" Or "Scf" Or "Thr"* (see Figure 27.6 opposite).
- Click in the **Validation Text** box and type *Enter Act, Com, Hor, Scf or Thr* (see Figure 27.6 opposite).
- Click on the **View** icon [圃] in the toolbar.
- Click on **Yes** to save the table.

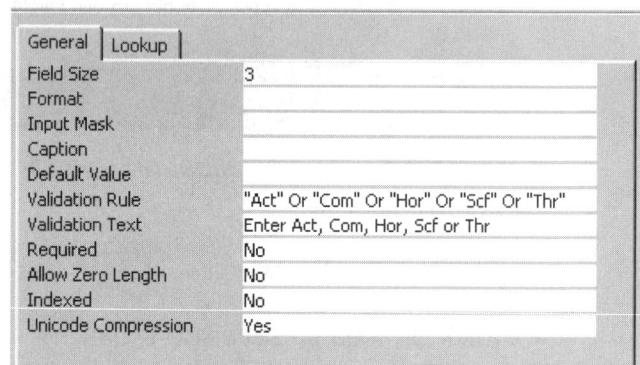

Figure 27.6: The validation rule for Category

The Videos table will be displayed. We are now ready to test the new validation rule.

- Click in the **Category** field for the first video, delete the current value and enter *Car.* The new validation rule should check this data and reject it as shown in Figure 27.7.

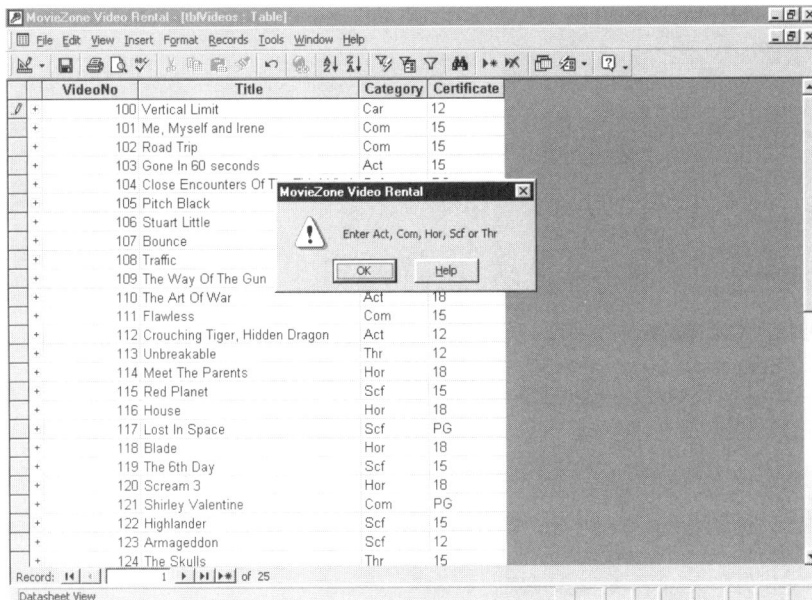

Figure 27.7: Testing the validation rule for Category

- Click on **OK** and change the **Category** for the first video back to *Act*.

The last validation rule specified in the Videos table design is that the **Certificate** field can only contain one of the values *U*, *PG*, *12*, *15* or *18*. To set up this validation rule follow the steps listed below.

- Click on the **Design** icon [Design] to open the Videos table in Design View.

- Click next to **Certificate** in the **Field Name** column.

- Click in the **Validation Rule** box and type *"U" Or "PG" Or "12" Or "15" Or "18"* (see Figure 27.8 opposite).

- Click in the **Validation Text** box and type *Only U, PG, 12, 15 or 18 are allowed* (see Figure 27.8 opposite).

- Click on the **View** icon [grid] in the toolbar.

- Click on **Yes** to save the table.

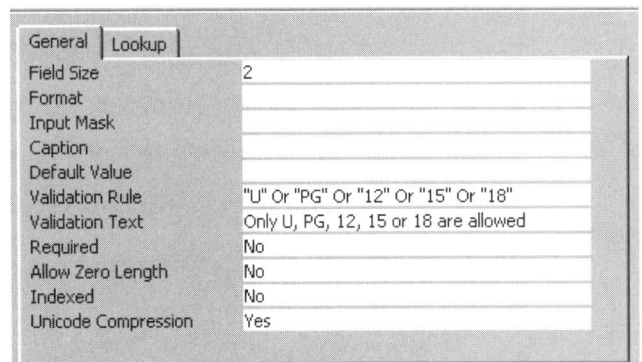

Figure 27.8: The validation rule for Certificate

The Videos table will be displayed. We are now ready to test the new validation rule.

- Click in the **Certificate** field for the first video, delete the current value and enter *21*. The new validation rule should check this data and reject it (Figure 27.9).

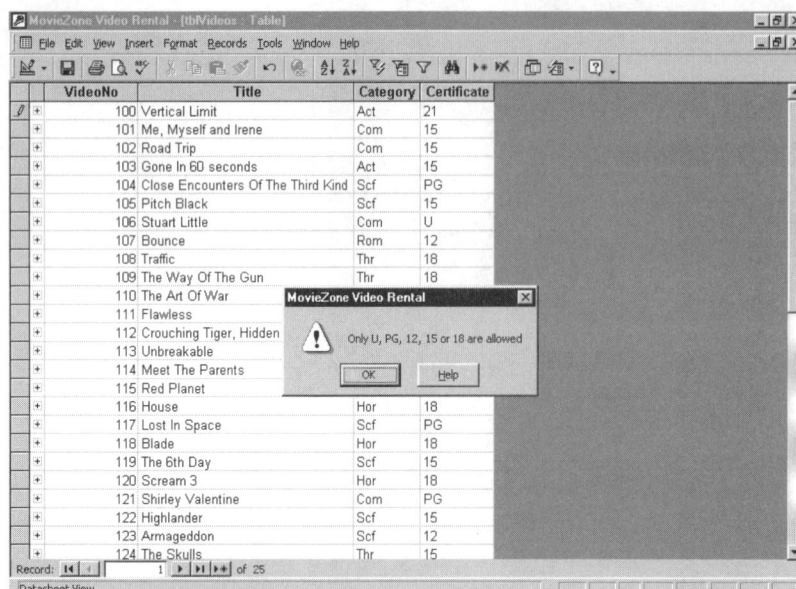

Figure 27.9: Testing the validation rule for Certificate

- Click on **OK** and change the **Certificate** for the first video back to *12*.
- Close the Videos table by clicking the **X** in the top right-hand corner of its window.

You have now set up all the validation checks specified in the Videos table design.

Task 27.4

Setting up data validation checks for the Loans table

The first validation rule in the Loans table design specifies that there must be a video with the same video number on the Videos table. Access will take care of this automatically so long as you specify **Enforce Referential Integrity** when you set up the relationship between the two tables. You did this on Page 120.

Similarly, the second validation rule for **MemberNo** (the member must exist on the Members table) is also taken care of by specifying **Enforce Referential Integrity** when you set up the relationship between the Members and Loans tables.

The third validation rule is that values in the **LengthofLoan** field can only be *1*, *2* or *3*.

- Start in the Database window and click on the **Tables** object type.
- Click on the **tblLoans** icon.
- Click on the **Design** icon ![Design] to open the table in Design View.

- Click next to **LengthofLoan** in the **Field Name** column.

- Click in the **Validation Rule** box and type *"1" Or "2" Or "3"* (see Figure 27.10).

- Click in the **Validation Text** box and type *Must be 1, 2, or 3 days* (see Figure 27.10).

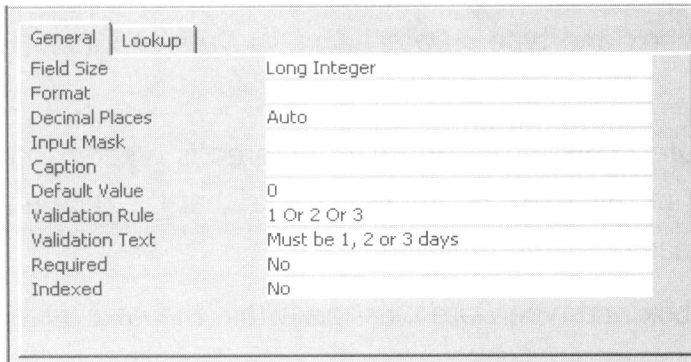

Figure 27.10: The validation rule for LengthofLoan

- Click on the **View** icon in the toolbar.

- Click on **Yes** to save the table.

The Loans table will be displayed. We are now ready to test the new validation rule.

- Click in the **LengthofLoan** field for the first loan, delete the current value and enter 9. The new validation rule should check this data and reject it as shown in Figure 27.11 below.

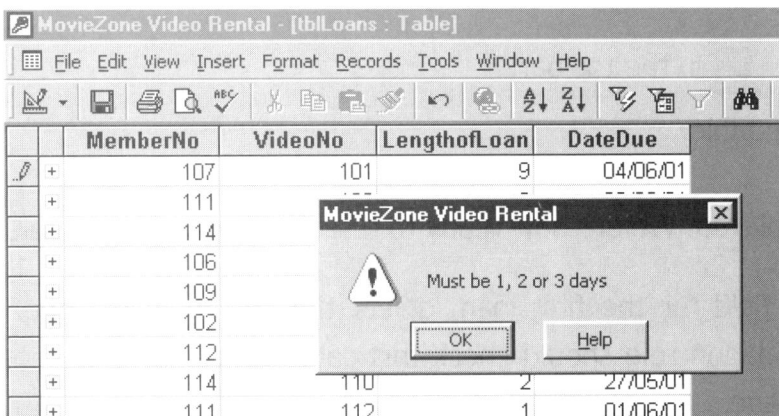

Figure 27.11: Testing the validation rule for LengthofLoan

- Click on **OK** and change the **LengthofLoan** for the first loan back to *2*.

The last validation rule specified in the Loans table design is that the **DateDue** field can only contain a date that is greater than the current date and no more than three days ahead. To set up this validation rule follow the steps listed below.

- Click on the **Design** icon [Design] to open the Videos table in Design View.
- Click next to **DateDue** in the **Field Name** column.
- Click in the **Validation Rule** box and type *>Date() And <=Date()+3* (see Figure 27.12 below).

    The first part of this rule *>Date()* checks that the date entered is greater than the current date. The second part of this rule *<=Date()+3* checks that the date entered is no more than three days ahead of the current date.

- Click in the **Validation Text** box and type *Date must be within the next three days* (see Figure 27.12 below).

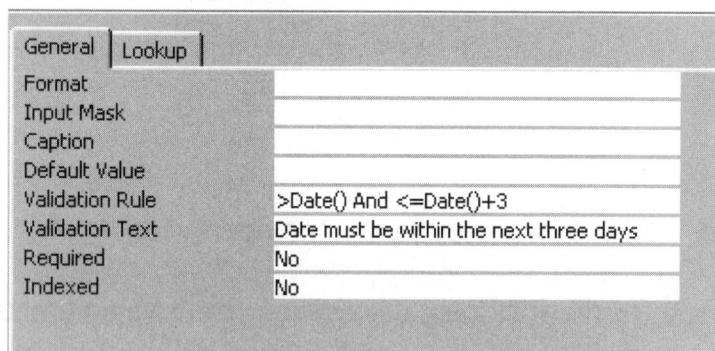

General	Lookup	
Format		
Input Mask		
Caption		
Default Value		
Validation Rule	>Date() And <=Date()+3	
Validation Text	Date must be within the next three days	
Required	No	
Indexed	No	

Figure 27.12: The validation rule for DateDue

- Click on the **View** icon [▦] in the toolbar.
- Click on **Yes** to save the table.

The Loans table will be displayed. We are now ready to test the new validation rule.

- Click in the **DateDue** field for the first loan, delete the current value and enter 24/10/01. The new validation rule should check this data and reject it as shown in Figure 27.13 over the page.

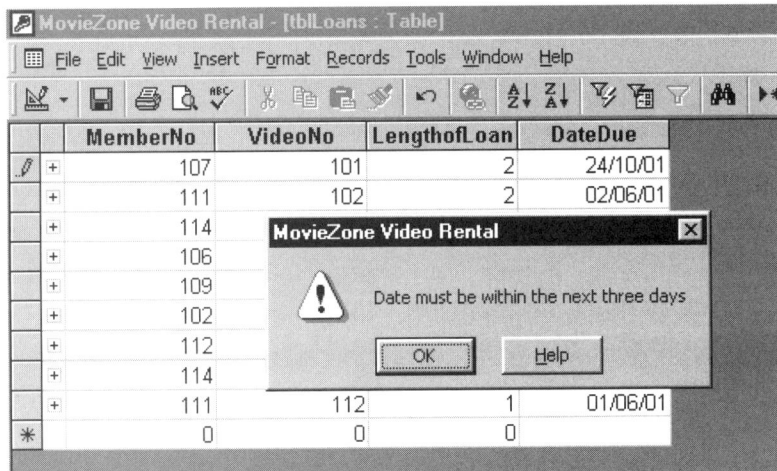

Figure 27.13: Testing the validation rule for DateDue

- Click on **OK**.

- Close the Loans table by clicking the **X** in the top right-hand corner of its window.

- Click on **Yes** when you see the message shown in Figure 27.14 below. This will close the Loans table without saving any of the changes to the first record.

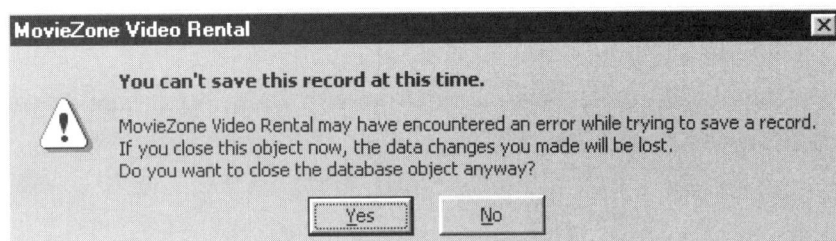

Figure 27.14: Closing the Loans table without saving changes

You have now set up all the validation checks specified in the Loans table design.

Chapter 28

Creating and using queries

This chapter describes how to create and use **queries**, which are used to search the data stored in tables to find records matching certain **search criteria** or **conditions**.

Task 28.1

Creating a query to search the Videos table

This task describes how to create a simple query which will be used to search the Videos table.

- Click on **Queries** in the Objects bar of the Database window.
- Double-click on the **Create query by using wizard** icon in the Database window.

The **Simple Query Wizard** window (Figure 28.1) will open.

- Click on the small down-arrow on the right-hand side of the **Tables/Queries** box and choose **tblVideos** from the list.

The next step is to choose the fields that you want to see in the finished query. In this case we want all of the fields in the Videos table to be displayed.

- To do this click on the right-facing double arrow next to the **Available Fields** box.

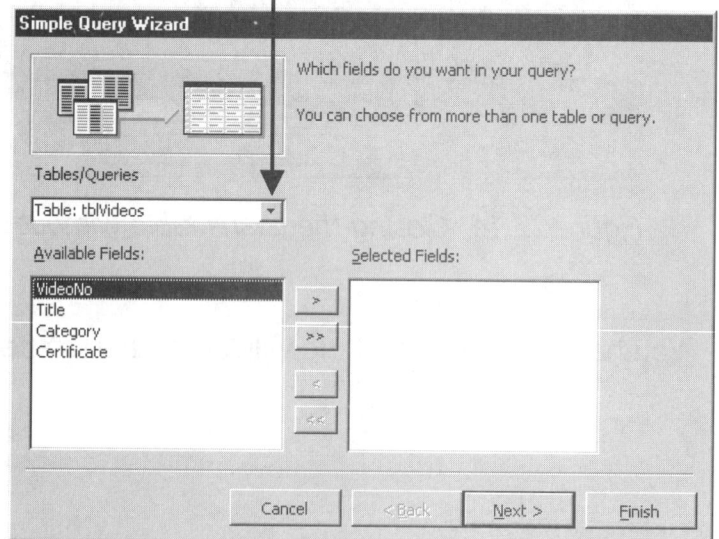

Figure 28.1: The simple query wizard window

- Click on **Next** and enter **qryVideos** as the title for the query.

164

- Choose **Modify the query design** and click on **Finish**.

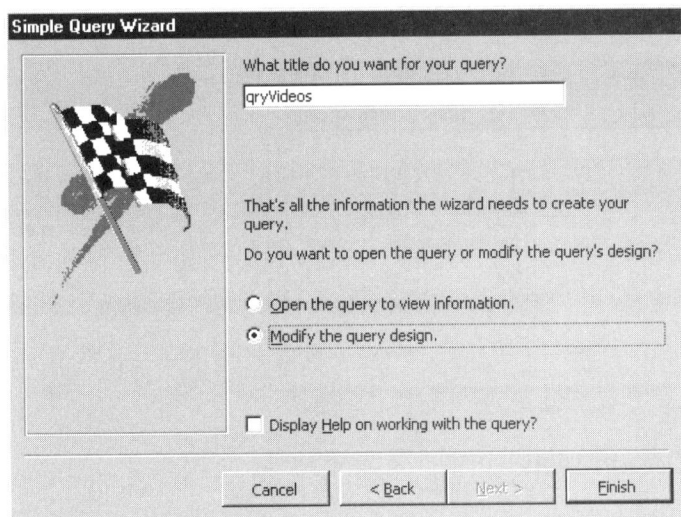

Figure 28.2: Giving a new query a title

The Query window will be opened in Design View – it should look something like the one shown below in Figure 28.3.

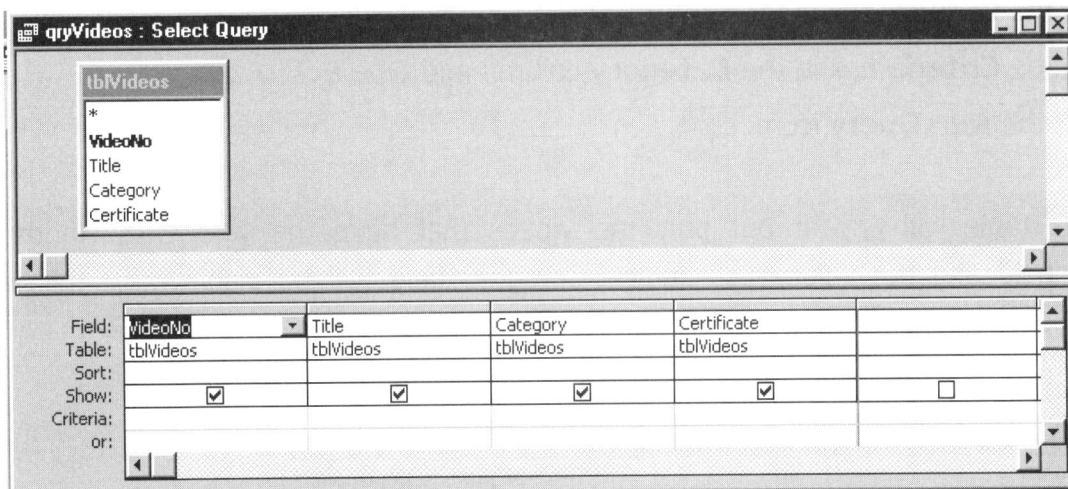

Figure 28.3: The Video query in Design View

Now we'll look at how this query can be used.

Suppose for example you needed to search for all the videos with an 18 certificate.

- Click in the **Criteria** box in the **Certificate** column and type *18*.
- Click on the **Run Query** icon.

- The Videos table will appear but only the videos that have the value "18" in the **Certificate** field will be displayed as shown in Figure 28.4 below.

qryVideos : Select Query

VideoNo	Title	Category	Certificate
108	Traffic	Thr	18
109	The Way Of The Gun	Thr	18
110	The Art Of War	Act	18
114	Meet The Parents	Hor	18
116	House	Hor	18
118	Blade	Hor	18
120	Scream 3	Hor	18

Record: 8 of 8

Figure 28.4: The video query in Design View

Next suppose that we needed to find all the Science Fiction videos with a 15 certificate. To do this we must search more than one field. This type of search is often known as a **complex search**.

- With the Videos query table still on the screen click on the **Design View** button.
- Click in the **Criteria** box in the **Certificate** column and type **15**
- Click in the **Criteria** box in the **Category** column and type **Scf**
- Click on the **Run Query** icon.

The Videos table will appear but only the videos that have the value "15" in the Certificate field and the value "Scf" in the Category field will be displayed – this is shown in Figure 28.5 below.

qryVideos : Select Query

VideoNo	Title	Category	Certificate
105	Pitch Black	Scf	15
115	Red Planet	Scf	15
119	The 6th Day	Scf	15
122	Highlander	Scf	15

Record: 1 of 4

Figure 28.5: Using a query to carry out a complex search

Exercise 28

Use the Videos query to search the video table and answer the following questions.

1. How many videos have a 15 certificate?
2. How many videos have a 12 certificate?
3. How many science fiction videos are there?
4. How many action videos are there?
5. How many science fiction videos have an 18 certificate?
6. How many comedy videos have a 15 certificate?

Task 28.2

Allowing users to enter search criteria

The query design for the MovieZone system states that the Video query will be used to find videos with the same:

- **category**

- **certificate**

- **category** <u>and</u> **certificate**

- **title**

In order to develop a user-friendly system we need to customise the Videos query so that users can enter their own criteria for each of these types of search without having to work in Design View. We will look at how this can be done by creating a customised version of the Video query that can be used to search for videos with the same category.

- With the Videos query table still on the screen click on the **Design View** button.

- Click in the **Criteria** box in the **Category** column and type *[Enter category]* as shown in Figure 28.6.

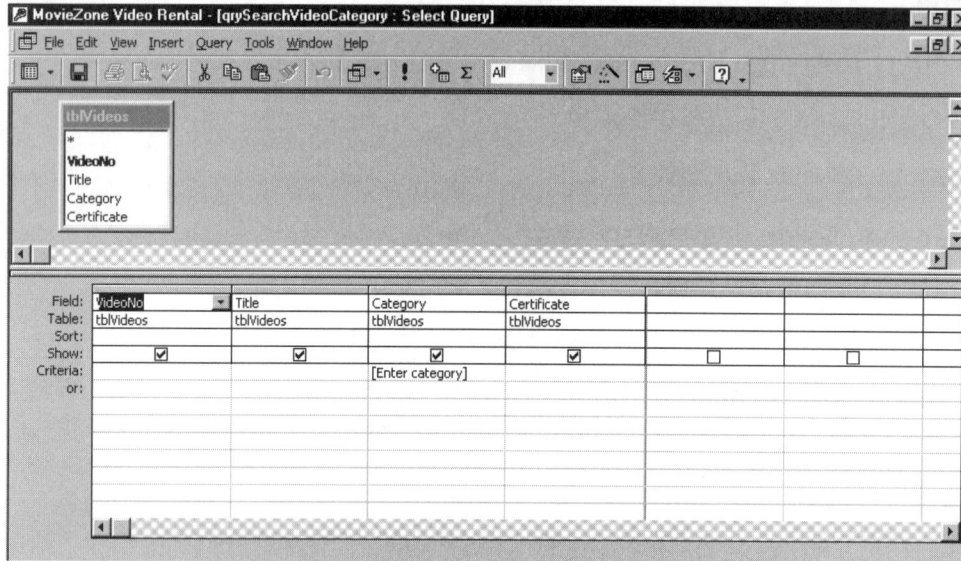

Figure 28.6: Customising a query

- Click on the **Run Query** icon. ▐!▌

  A window will appear (Figure 28.7) with the message that you entered in the square brackets.

- Type *scf* and click **OK**. The query will find all the videos in the science fiction (scf) category.

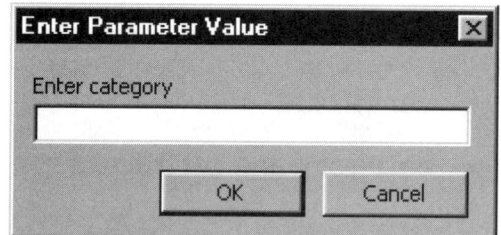

Figure 28.7: Running the query

We will save this version of the videos query with a new name so that it can be used to carry out this particular type of search again.

- Click on **File**, **Save As** and enter *qrySearchVideoCategory* (Figure 28.8).

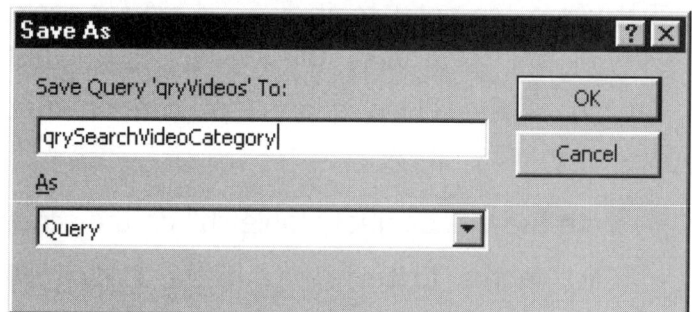

Figure 28.8: Saving a copy of the query

- Close the query by clicking the **X** in the top right-hand corner of its window.

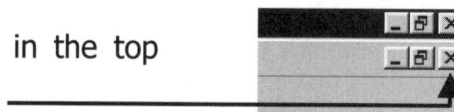

Next we will use exactly the same method to create a customised version of the video query that can be used to search for videos with the same certificate.

- Start in the Database window and click on the **Queries** object type.
- Click on the **qryVideos** icon.
- Click on the **Design** icon [Design] to open the table in Design View.
- Click in the **Criteria** box in the **Certificate** column and type *[Enter certificate]*.
- Click on the **Run Query** icon. [!]
- Type *18* and click **OK**.

  The query will find all the certificate 18 videos.

- Click on **File**, **Save As** and enter *qrySearchVideoCertificate*.
- Close the query by clicking the **X** in the top right-hand corner of its window.

Next we will use exactly the same method to create a customised version of the video query that can be used to search for videos with a particular title.

- Start in the Database window and click on the **Queries** object type.
- Click on the **qryVideos** icon.
- Click on the **Design** icon [Design] to open the table in Design View.
- Click in the **Criteria** box in the **Title** column and type *[Enter title]*.
- Click on the **Run Query** icon. [!]
- Type *Bounce* and click **OK**.

  The query will find all the videos with this title.

- Click on **File**, **Save As** and enter *qrySearchVideoTitle*.
- Close the query by clicking the **X** in the top right-hand corner of its window.

Finally we will create a customised version of the video query that can be used to search for videos with the same category and certificate.

- Start in the Database window and click on the **Queries** object type.
- Click on the **qryVideos** icon.
- Click on the **Design** icon [Design] to open the table in Design View.
- Click in the **Criteria** box in the **Category** column and type *[Enter category]*.

- Click in the **Criteria** box in the **Certificate** column and type *[Enter certificate]*.

- Click on the **Run Query** icon. ⚠️

- Type *com* and click **OK**.

  Type *15* and click **OK**.

  The query will find all the certificate 15 comedy (com) videos.

- Click on **File**, **Save As** and enter *qrySearchVideoCategoryCertificate*.

- Close the query by clicking the **X** in the top right-hand corner of its window.

Task 28.3

Creating a query to find overdue videos

- Start in the Database window and click on the **Queries** object type.

- Double-click on the **Create query by using wizard** icon.

The Simple Query Wizard window will open.

- Click on the small down-arrow on the right of the **Tables/Queries** box and click on **tblMembers** in the list.

- Move every field <u>except</u> **MemberNo** and **DateOfBirth** across to the **Selected Fields** box by clicking on the field name in the **Available Fields** box and the right-facing single arrow `>` next to it (Figure 28.9).

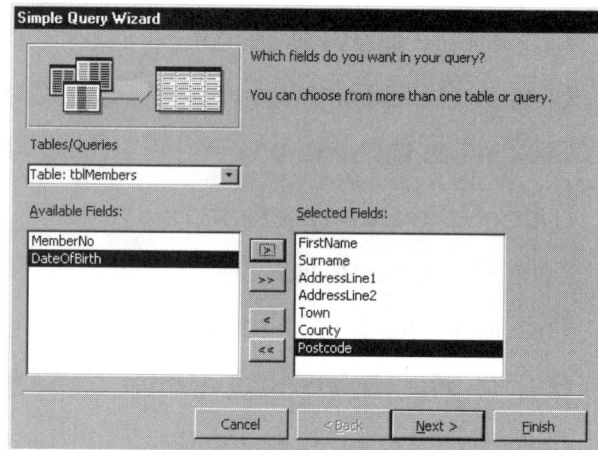

Figure 28.9: Selecting fields for a query

- Click the small down-arrow on the right of the **Tables/Queries** box and click on **tblLoans** in the list.

- Move the **VideoNo** and **DateDue** fields across to the **Selected Fields** box as described above.

- Click the small down-arrow on the right of the **Tables/Queries** box and click on **tblVideos** in the list.

- Move the **Title** field across to the **Selected Fields** box as described above.

- Click **Next** <u>twice</u>.

- Enter **qryOverdue** as the title for the query.

- Choose **Modify the query design** and click **Finish**.

The new query will be displayed in Design View. To finish off this query we need to enter the search criteria to find the overdue videos. Follow the steps below to do this.

- Use the scroll bar at the bottom of the query to move across to the right until you can see the column for the **DateDue** field.

- Enter *<Date()* in the **Criteria** box for this field (Figure 28.10). This will make the query find videos with a DateDue earlier than the system date on your computer.

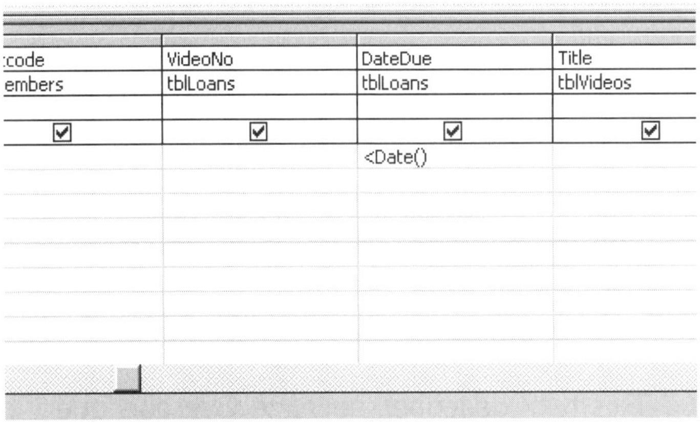

Figure 28.10: Entering search criteria for a query

Finally all we need to do now is move the **Title** column so that it is before the **DateDue** and after the **VideoNo** – this is just a more sensible order and will save us some time when we come to set up the overdue videos report.

- Click on the thin grey bar above **Title** to highlight the whole column (Figure 28.11).

- Rest the white pointer arrow at the top of the **Title** column.

- Click and hold the left mouse button.

- Drag the **Title** column to the left and drop it between the **VideoNo** and **DateDue** columns by letting go of the mouse button (Figure 28.12).

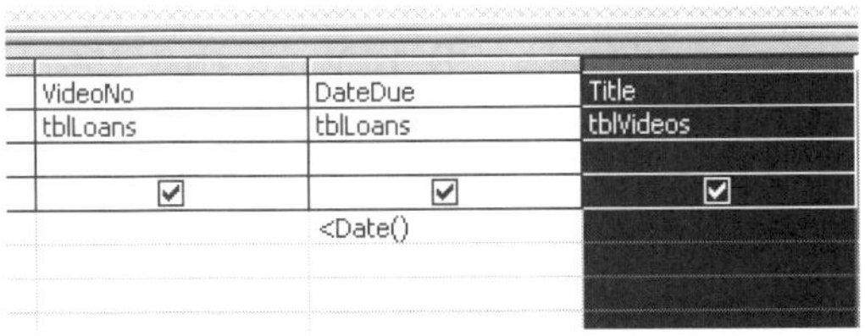

Figure 28.11: Selecting a column

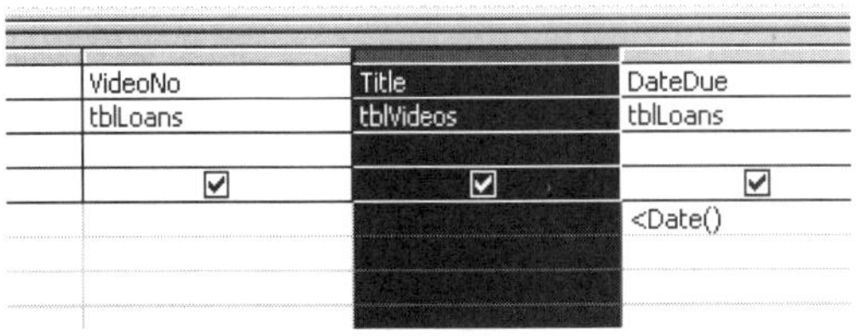

Figure 28.12: Moving a column

- Click on the **Run Query** icon.

The query will display the details of all the overdue videos. You will need to scroll across the screen to see all of the information — this is isn't anything to be concerned about because we are going to create a report to display this information more clearly.

- Close the query by clicking the **X** in the top right-hand corner of its window.
- Click **Yes** to save changes to the query design.

You have now created all of the queries needed for the MovieZone system. Next we will look at how the Overdue query can be used to generate overdue reminder letters.

Task 28.4

Using the Overdue query to generate reminder letters

This task describes how the Overdue query can be used to create a standard letter in MS Word, which can be used in a mail-merge to generate personalised letters for members with overdue videos.

- Start in the Database window and click on the **Queries** object type.
- Click once on the **qryOverdue** icon.
- Click **Tools, Office Links, Merge It with MS Word** (Figure 28.13).

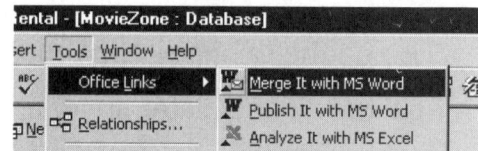

Figure 28.13

- Choose **Create a new document and then link the data to it**, and click **OK**.
- MS Word will be loaded and then minimized. Switch to the new Word document by clicking on its icon at the bottom of the screen (Figure 28.14). If the MS Word window doesn't fill the screen, click the **Maximize** button ⬜ in its top right-hand corner.

Figure 28.14

- Type the standard Overdue Reminder letter exactly as shown in Figure 28.14 below. The positions where data from the Overdue query will be inserted in the mail-merge d letters are contained within « » symbols – wherever you see these symbols click **Insert Merge Field** on the toolbar and choose the field you need from the drop-down list.

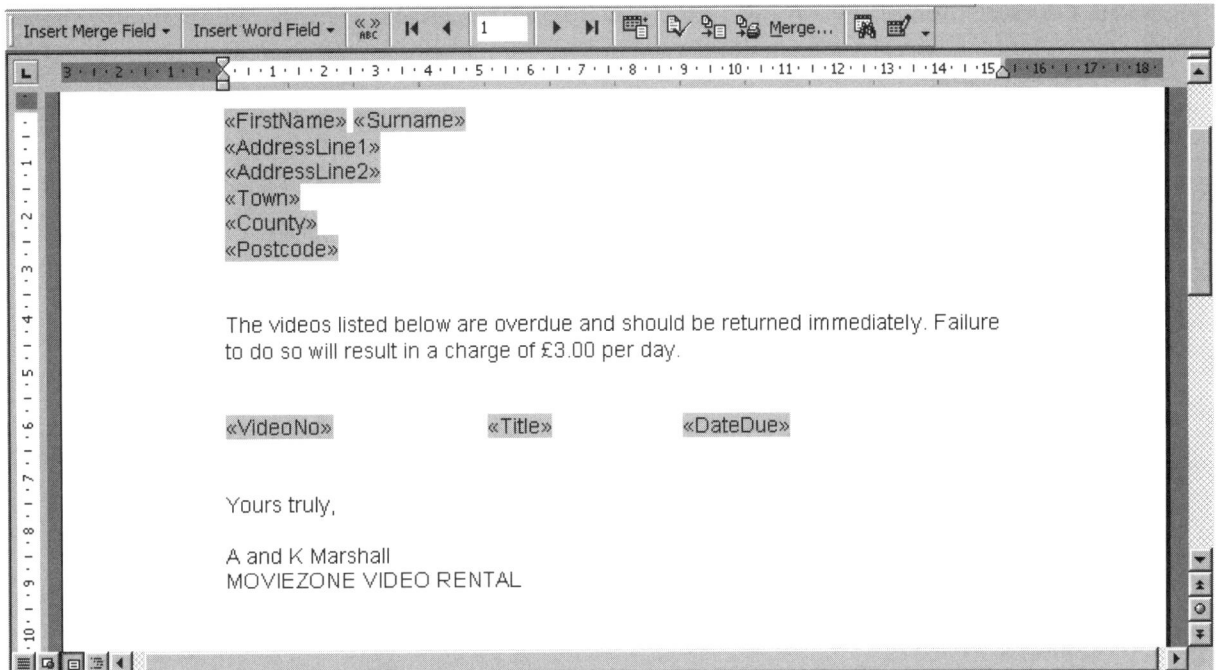

Figure 28.15: The standard Overdue Reminder letter

- To preview a standard letter with data inserted click the **View Merged Data** icon on the Mail Merge toolbar at the top of the screen.
- To generate and print a complete set of letters click on the **Merge to Printer** icon on the Mail Merge toolbar at the top of the screen – <u>don't do this</u> unless you really do want a set of personalised overdue letters!
- Click **File**, **Save As** in the Menu bar.
- Enter *OverdueLetter* as the filename and click **Save**.

In the next chapter we will look at how to create and customise a report to present the information found by the Overdue query.

Chapter 29

Creating and customising reports

This chapter describes how to generate a report based on a query and customise it.

Task 29.1

Creating a report to list overdue videos

- Click on **Reports** in the Objects bar of the Database window.
- Double-click on **Create report by using wizard**.
- Click the down-arrow on the right-hand side of the **Tables/Queries** box and choose **qryOverdue** from the list (Figure 29.1). ──────┐
- Move **all** of the fields into the **Selected Fields** box by clicking on the right-facing double arrow `>>` next to the **Available Fields** box.
- Click on **Next**.

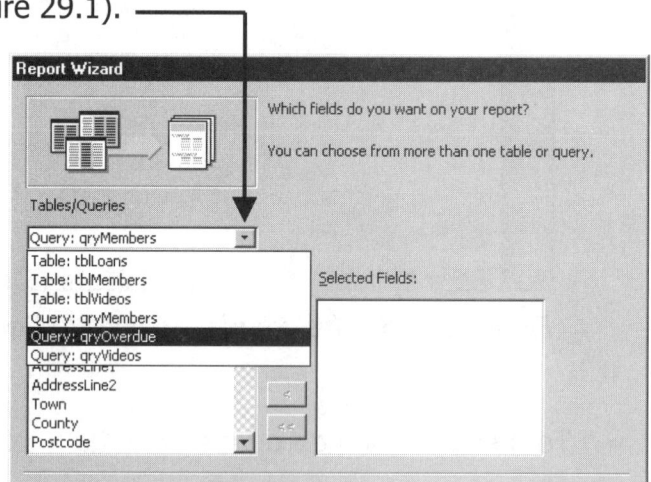

Figure 29.1: Creating the Overdue Videos report

- The next dialogue box will ask how you want to view your data. Choose **tblMembers** from the list and click **Next**.
- Click **Next** _three_ times to skip through the next few windows.
- The next dialogue box will ask how you want to lay out your report. Choose **Outline 1** for **Layout**.
- Click on **Next** _twice_.
- Enter _rptOverdue_ as the title for the report.
- Choose **Modify the report's design**, and click **Finish**.

- The Overdue Videos report will be displayed – it should look something like the one shown below in Figure 29.2.

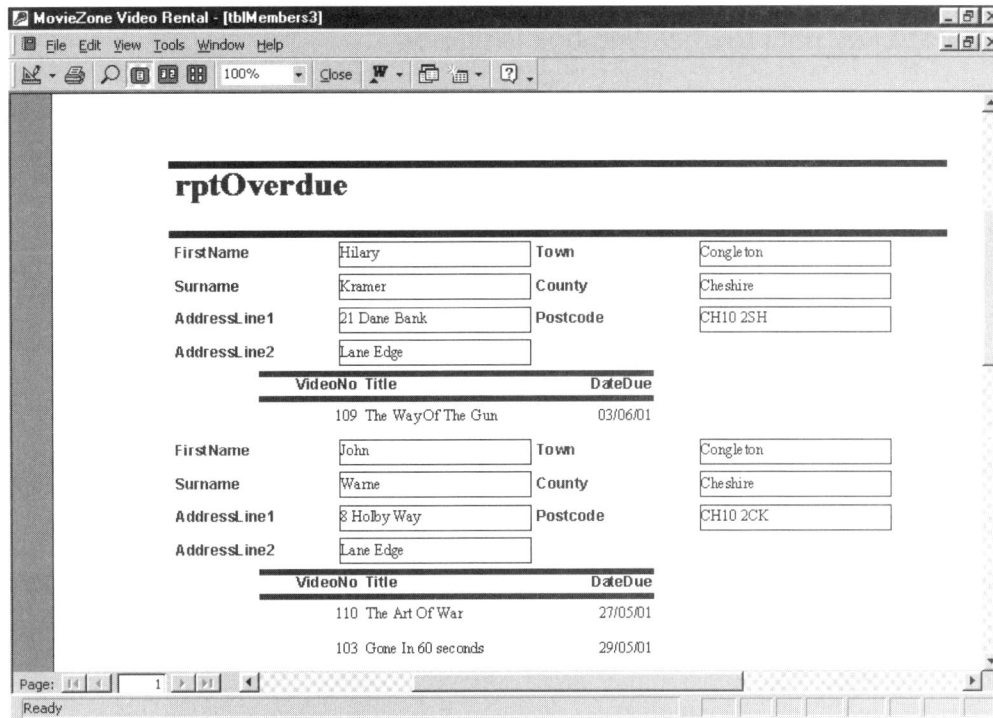

Figure 29.2: The Overdue Videos report for 4th June 2001 before

Next we need to change the layout and format of this report so that it matches the design shown on page 85. The next task describes the steps that must be followed to do this.

Task 29.2

Customising the overdue videos report

- Click on the **Design** icon [Design] to open the report in Design View.

- Click on **Reports** in the Objects bar of the Database window.

- Double-click on the **rptOverdue** icon.

- Click **Edit, Select All** and change the font to **Arial**.

- Click on any blank white area of the form to deselect everything.

In the **Report Header** section:

- Click on the heading **rptOverdue**.

- Press the **Delete** key until the heading box is empty.

- Enter *Overdue Videos*.

- Click anywhere in the **Report Header** section away from the heading.

- Click once on the heading to reselect it.

- Increase the size of the heading box until all of the text can be seen (Figure 29.3).

Figure 29.3: Changing the size of the report header text box

- Now rest the mouse pointer on the edge of the heading box until you see a hand shape. Click and hold the left mouse button. Drag the heading box down slightly and let go of the mouse button.

In the **First Name Header** section:

- Rest the mouse pointer on the gray bar labelled **Detail** until you see this shape.

- Click and hold the left mouse button

- Drag down to increase the size of the **First Name Header** section until it is approximately the same size as the one on the report in Figure 29.4 below.

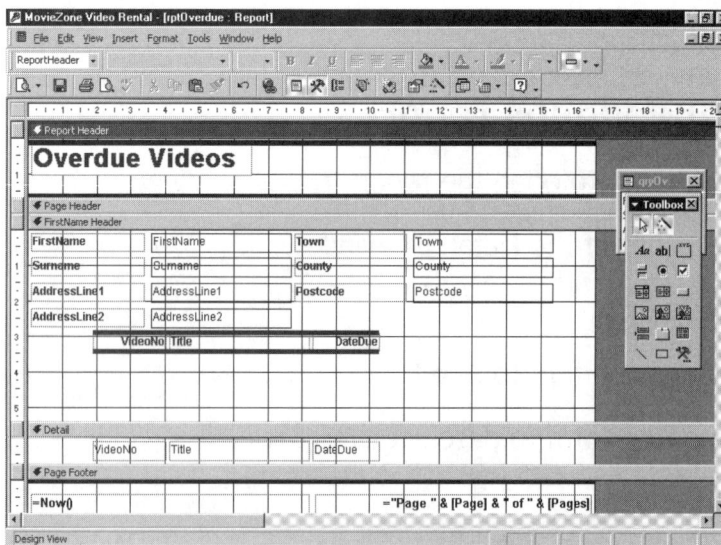

Figure 29.4: Increasing the size of a section

- Hold the **Shift** ⬆ key and click on each field name label in turn until they are all selected as shown in Figure 29.5.

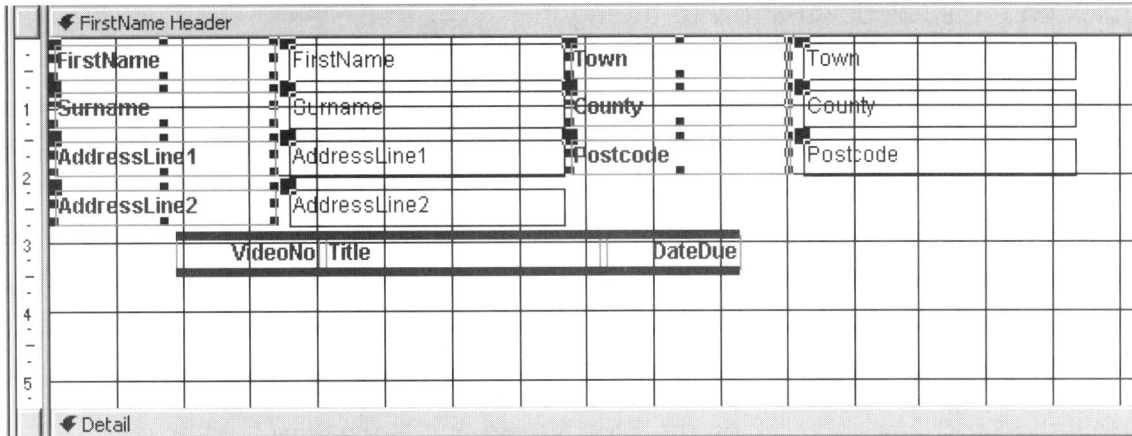

Figure 29.5: Selecting all of the field name labels

- Click on the **Cut** button ✄ on the Formatting toolbar to remove the field name labels.

- Hold the **Shift** key and click on part of the video details heading as shown in Figure 29.6 opposite.

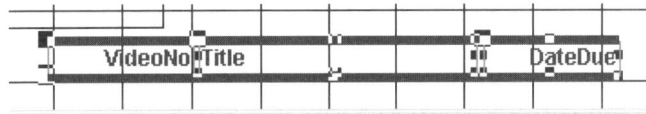

Figure 29.6

- Click on the **Cut** button ✄ on the Formatting toolbar to remove all these items. If anything is left behind just use the **Shift** key to select and the **Cut** button to remove it.

- Reposition the field boxes by clicking on them one at a time and dragging and dropping until they are arranged like the ones shown below in Figure 29.7.

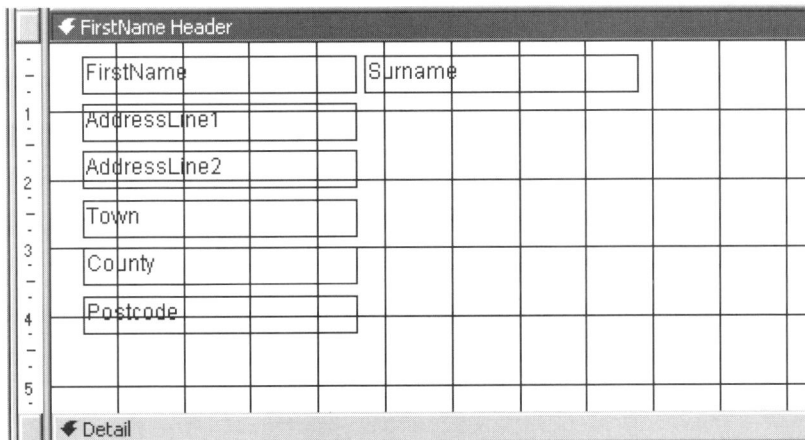

Figure 29.7: The repositioned field boxes

- Hold the **Shift** key and click on each of the field boxes in turn until they are all selected.

- Click on the small down-arrow to the right of the **Line/Border Color** button on the Formatting toolbar and choose **Transparent** (Figure 29.8).

  This will make the lines around the field boxes invisible on the finished report.

Figure 29.8

- Click on any blank white area of the form to deselect the field boxes.

- Hold the **Shift** key and click on the **FirstName** and **Surname** field boxes.

- Click the **Bold** text button **B** on the Formatting toolbar.

In the **Detail** section:

- Click on the **VideoNo** field box and drag it to the left until it is lined up with the field boxes in the **First Name Header** section. Click on the **Align Left** button on the Formatting toolbar.

- Click on **Title** and drag it to the left until it is next to **VideoNo**.

- Click on the **DateDue** field box and drag it two squares to the right.

- Click on **Title** and increase the size of the field box so that it ends just before **DateDue**.

When you have made these changes the **Detail** section of the form should look like the one shown below in Figure 29.9.

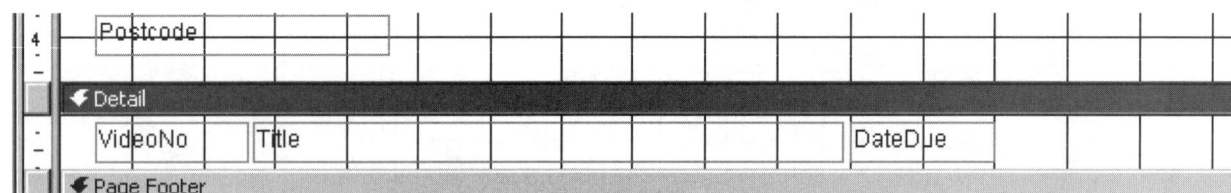

Figure 29.9: The Detail section of the form after changes

We have now made all of the changes needed to make the report match its design.

- Click on the **View** button. Your report should look something like the one shown in Figure 29.10 below.

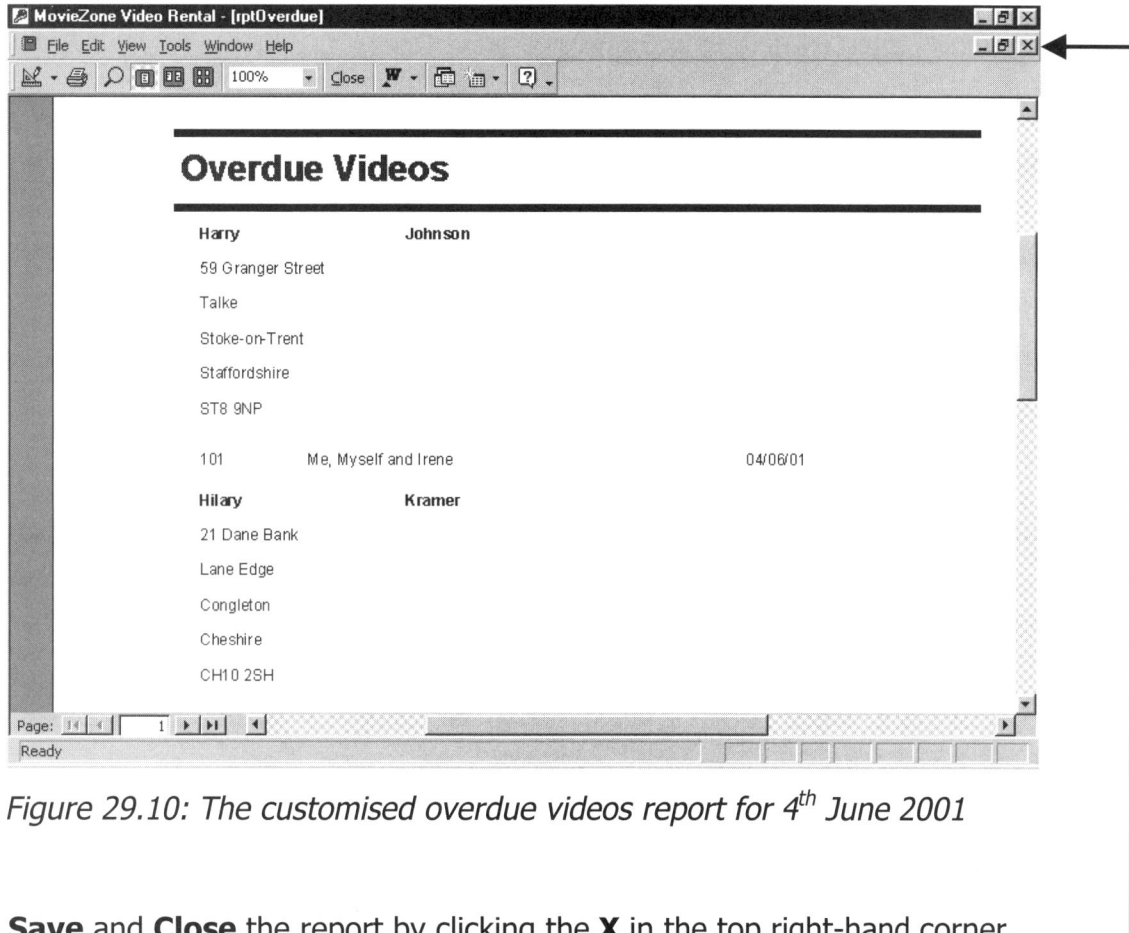

Figure 29.10: The customised overdue videos report for 4th June 2001

- **Save** and **Close** the report by clicking the **X** in the top right-hand corner.
- Click **Yes** to save changes to the report design.

Chapter 30

Creating the menu system

This chapter describes how to set up a menu-driven user interface with **menu forms** and **command buttons**. An alternative method would be to use **switchboards**. This is not explained here because it is not always available in versions of Access 2000 running on school or college networks.

Task 30.1

Creating the Main menu form

Two menu forms were designed in Chapter 19. The first of these was the **Main menu**. This will provide a way for users to move easily between the Members, Videos and Loans data entry forms. This task describes how to create the menu form.

- Click on **Forms** in the Objects bar of the Database window.

- Double-click on **Create form in Design View**.

  A new blank form like the one shown in Figure 30.1 opposite will be created.

- If the form doesn't fill the screen click on the **Maximize** button ☐ in its top right-hand corner.

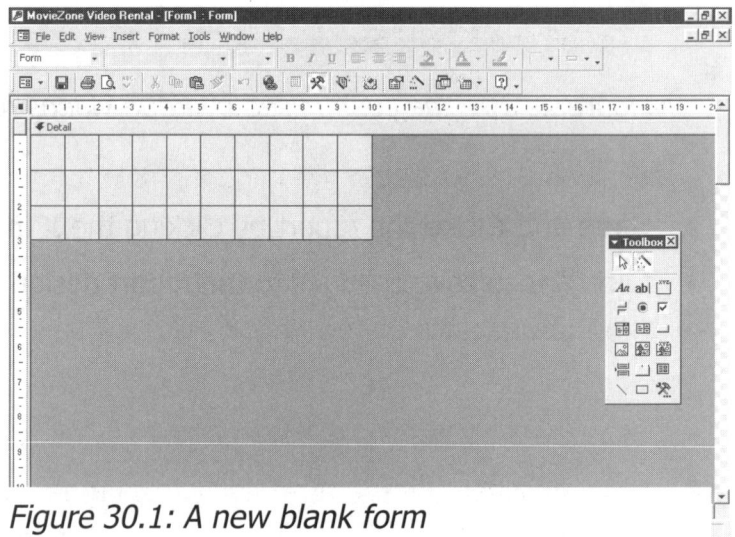

Figure 30.1: A new blank form

- Make the **Detail** area of the form larger by resting the mouse pointer on its bottom right-hand corner until it changes into this shape.

- Click and hold the left mouse button then drag down and across the screen to the right as shown in Figure 30.2 below.

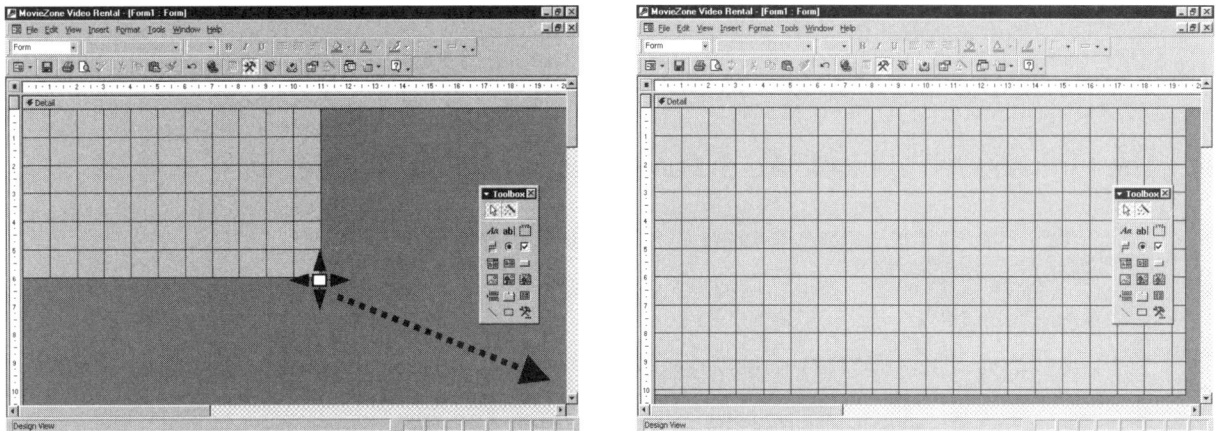

Figure 30.2: Making the working area of a form larger

First we need to add some headings to the form.

- Click on the **Label** tool *Aa* on the toolbox.

The pointer will change to a ^+A shape.

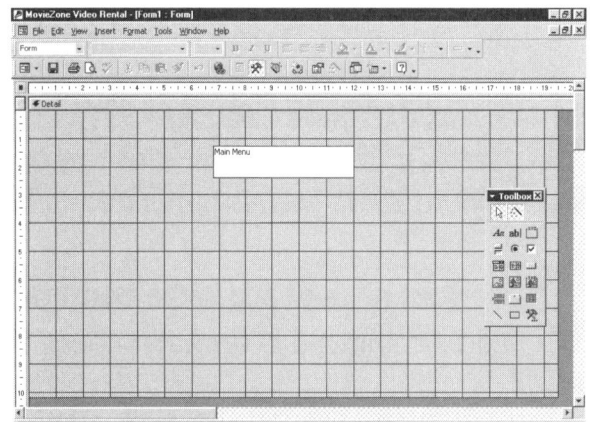

- Position the pointer in the middle of the form towards the top.

- Click and hold the left mouse button. Drag down and across to the right to open a label box.

- Type the heading *MovieZone*.

- Click anywhere on the form away from the label box.

Figure 30.3: Adding a text label to a form

Now we need to change the font type and size to the ones specified in the design for this form on page 90.

- Click on the label box to select it.

- Change the font to **Arial**, **48 point**, **bold** and **italic**.

Next we need to add another heading.

- Click on the **Label** tool and drag out another box underneath the *MovieZone* heading.

- Type the heading *Main Menu*.

- Click anywhere on the form away from the label box.

- Click on the label box to select it.

- Change the font to **Arial**, **36 point**, **bold**.

The form should now look like the one shown in Figure 30.4 below.

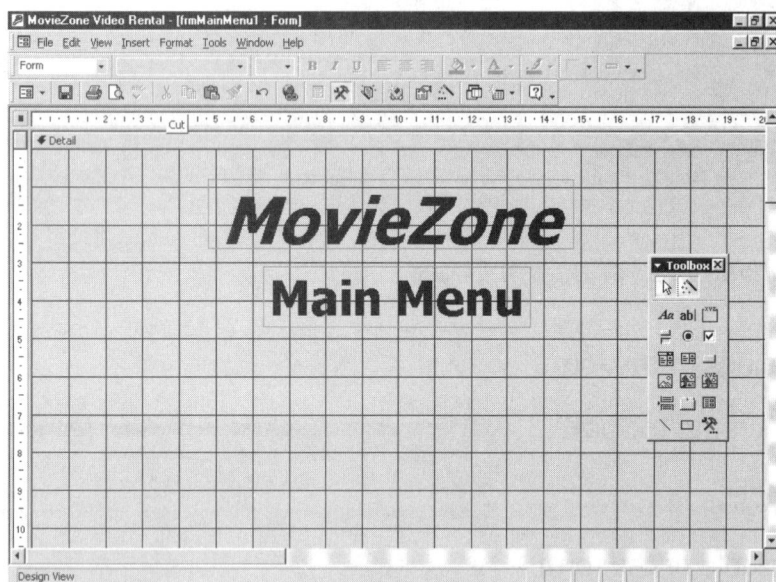

Figure 30.4: The Main menu form with text labels added

Now we need to add some **command buttons** to the form. First we will look at how to add a command button that opens the Loans form when it is clicked.

- Click on the **Command Button** tool ▭ on the toolbox.

The pointer will change to a $+_{\sqsubset}$ shape.

- Position the pointer in the middle of the form towards the left.

- Click and hold the left mouse button. Drag down and across to the right to create a command button. The **Command Button Wizard** will start up (Figure 30.5).

Note: If it doesn't, check that **Control Wizards** ▨ is selected in the toolbox.

- Select **Form Operations** in the **Categories** list box and **Open Form** in the **Actions** list box. This tells Access that we want this command button to open a form when it is clicked.

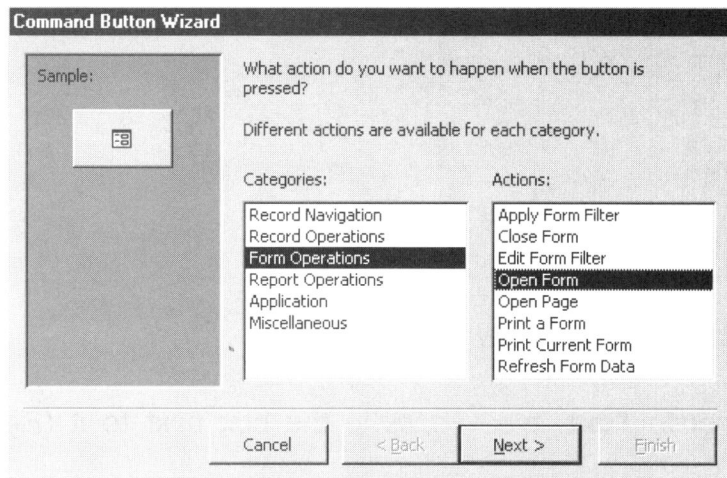

Figure 30.5: The Command button Wizard

- Click **Next**.

- A list of forms will be displayed. Choose **frmLoans** and click **Next** (Figure 30.6).

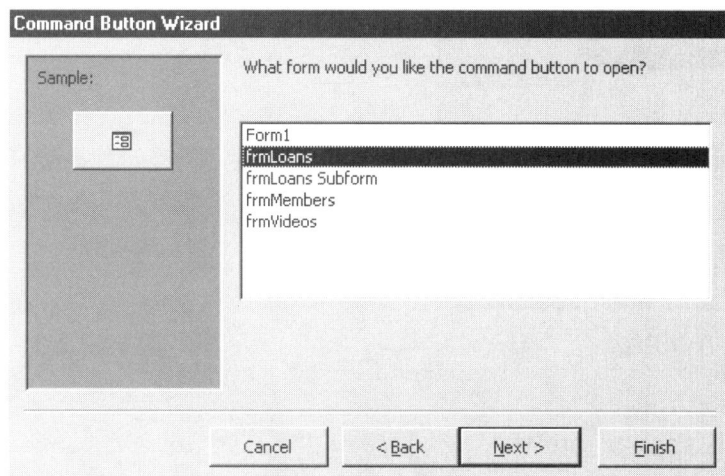

Figure 30.6: Choosing the form to open

- In the next dialogue box choose **Open the form and show all the records**, and click **Next** (Figure 30.7).

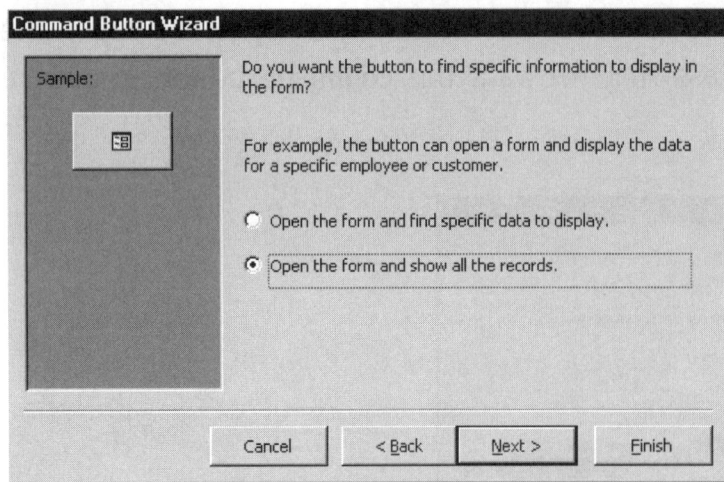

Figure 30.7: Specifying how a form should be opened

- In the next dialogue box choose **Text**, type *Loans* in the box next to it (Figure 30.8), and click **Finish**.

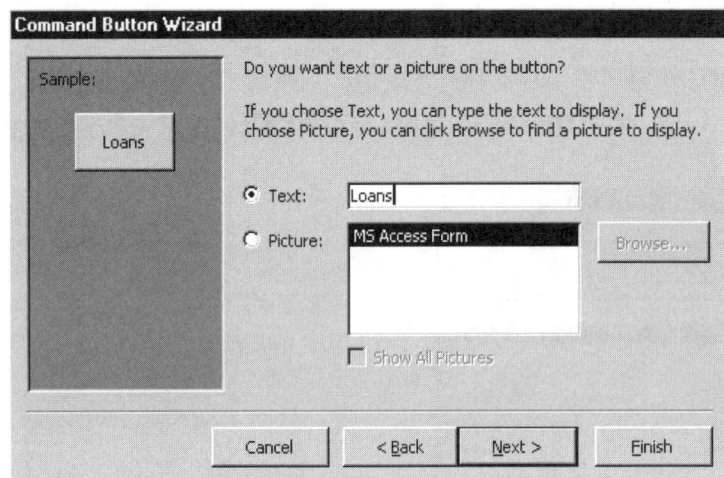

Figure 30.8: Labelling a command button

The new command button will appear on the screen. It should already be selected as shown in Figure 30.9 – if it isn't just click <u>once</u> on it.

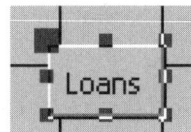

Figure 30.9: The Loans command button

- With the command button selected change the font to **Arial**, **18 point** and **bold** – this is the text format specified for this button in the Menu form design.

- You may need to change the size of the command button so that the text fits inside it. (Figure 30.10)

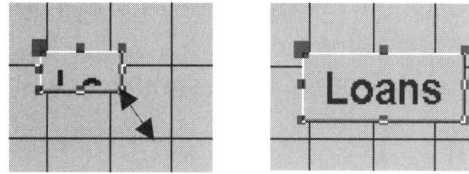

Figure 30.10: Resizing a command button

Now add two more command buttons to open the Videos form and the Members form. Do this in the same way as described above. The **Videos** button will open **frmVideos**, and the **Members** button will open **frmMembers**.

Next we need to add a command button that closes the system down when it is clicked.

- Click on the **Command Button** tool on the toolbox.
- Position the pointer underneath the Members command button.
- Click and hold the left mouse button. Drag down and across to the right to create a command button. The **Command Button Wizard** will start up.
- Select **Application** in the **Categories** list box and **Quit Application** in the **Actions** list box, then click **Next**.
- In the next dialogue box choose **Text**, type *Quit* in the box next to it, and click **Finish**.
- Change the font on the command button to **Arial**, **18 point** and **bold**.

You have now created all the command buttons needed on the Main menu form. The buttons might need lining up. The quickest way to do this is described below.

- Click on the Loans command button and hold down the **Shift** key.
- Keep hold of the **Shift** key and click on the Videos and Members command buttons. All three buttons should now be selected as shown in Figure 30.11 below.

Figure 30.11: Selecting more than one object

- Click on **Format**, **Align** and **Top**.

The Main menu form should now look something like the one shown in Figure 30.12 below.

Figure 30.12: The completed main menu form in Design View

All we need to do now is remove some of the standard lines and boxes that would normally appear on a data entry form – these are not needed on a menu form.

- Click on **View** and **Properties**.

A window will appear showing the properties for the form (Figure 30.13).

- Click on the **Format** tab if it isn't already selected.

- Change the setting for **Record Selectors** to **No**.

- Change the setting for **Navigation Buttons** to **No**.

- Change the setting for **Dividing Lines** to **No**.

Figure 30.13: Form format properties

Close the Main menu form by clicking the **X** in the top right-hand corner of its window.

- Click on **Yes** to save changes to the design of the form.

- Enter *frmMainMenu* as the form name.

Now that we have created the Main menu we can go on and create the Find Videos menu in exactly the same way.

Task 30.2

Creating the Find Videos menu form

The second menu form is the **Find Videos Menu**. This will offer the options available for searching through the information in the video table. This task describes how to create this menu form.

- Click on **Forms** in the Objects bar of the Database window.

- Double-click on **Create form in Design View** to create a new blank form.

- A new blank form will be created. If the form doesn't fill the screen click on the **Maximize** button in its top right-hand corner.

- Make the working area of the form larger by resting the mouse pointer on its bottom right-hand corner, holding down on the left mouse button and dragging down and across the screen to the right.

First we need to add a heading to the form.

- Click on the **label tool** *Aa* on the toolbox.
- Position the pointer in the middle of the form towards the top.
- Click and hold the left mouse button. Drag down and across to the right to open a label box.
- Type the heading *Find Videos*.
- Click anywhere on the form away from the label box.
- Click on the label box to select it.
- Change the font to **Arial, 26 point, bold**.

Now we need to add some **command buttons** to the form that will run queries when they are clicked. First we will look at how to add a command button to run the query that finds videos in a certain category.

- Click on the **Command Button** tool ▢ on the toolbox.
- Position the pointer on the left-hand side of the form underneath the heading.
- Click and hold the left mouse button. Drag down and across to the right to create a command button. The **Command Button Wizard** will start up.

- Select **Miscellaneous** in the **Categories** list box and **Run Query** in the **Actions** list box then click **Next** (Figure 30.14).

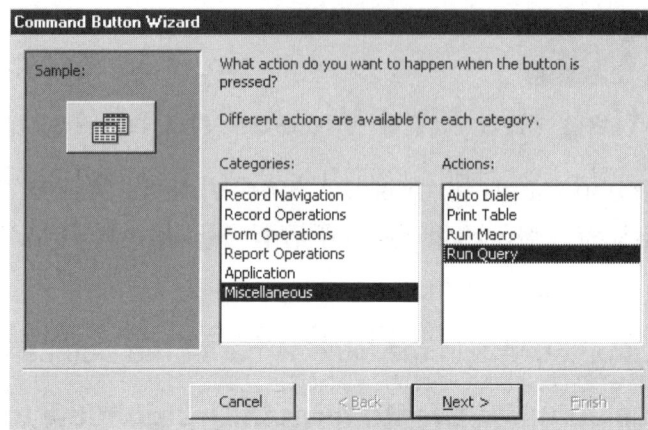

Figure 30.14: Running a query with a command button

- Choose **qrySearchVideoCategory** from the list of queries and click **Next** (Figure 30.15).

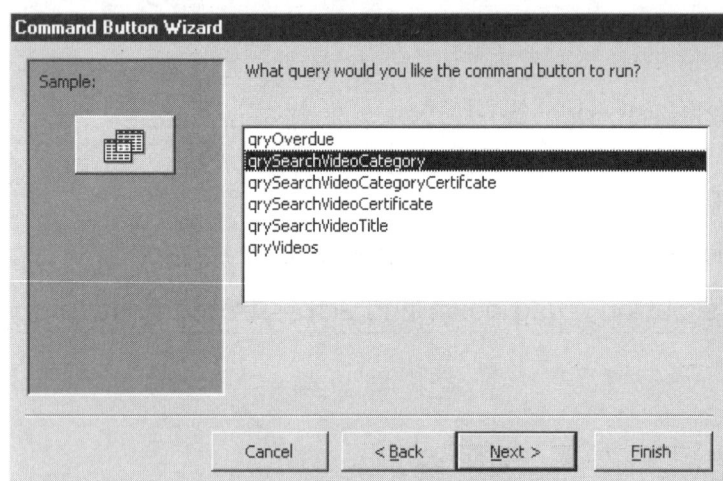

Figure 30.15: Choosing the query to run

- In the next dialogue box choose **Text**, type *Category* in the box next to it (Figure 30.16), and click **Finish**.

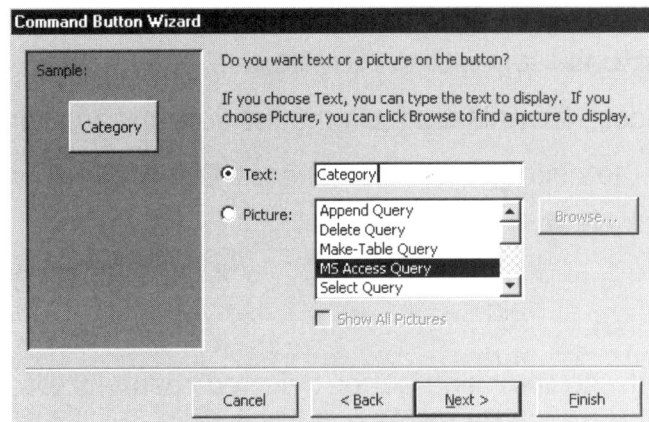

Figure 30.16: Labelling a query command button

- With the command button selected change the font to **Arial**, **18 point**, **bold**.
- Change the size of the command button so that the text fits inside it.

Now use the same method to add command buttons labelled **Certificate**, **Category and Certificate**, **Title**. These will run the queries **qrySearchVideoCertificate**, **qrySearchVideoCategoryCertificate** and **qrySearchVideoTitle**.

The command buttons might need lining up. The quickest way to do this is described below.

- Click on the **Category** command button and hold down the **Shift** key.
- Keep hold of the **Shift** key and click each of the other command buttons in turn. All four buttons should now be selected as shown in Figure 30.17 opposite.
- Click on **Format**, **Align** and **Left**.

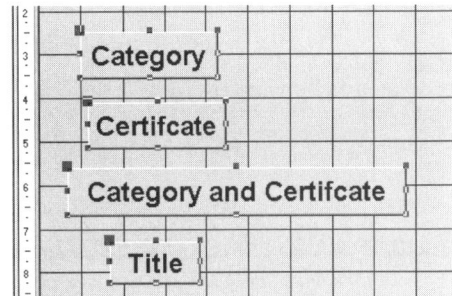

Figure 30.17: Lining up objects

Now we need to add a command button that allows users to go back to the previous menu by opening the **Videos** form.

- Click the **Command Button** tool on the toolbox.
- Position the pointer in the bottom right-hand corner of the form.
- Click and hold the left mouse button. Drag down and across to the right to create a command button. The **Command Button Wizard** will start up.

- Select **Form Operations** in the **Categories** list box and **Open Form** in the **Actions** list box then click **Next**.

- Choose **frmVideos** from the list of forms and click **Next**.

- In the next dialogue box choose **Open the form and show all the records**, and click **Next**.

- In the next dialogue box choose **Text**, type *Go Back* in the box next to it, and click **Finish**.

- With the command button selected change the font to **Arial**, **18 point**, **bold**.

- Change the size of the command button so that the text fits inside it.

You have now created all of the text labels and command buttons needed on this menu form which should now look something like the one shown below in Figure 30.18.

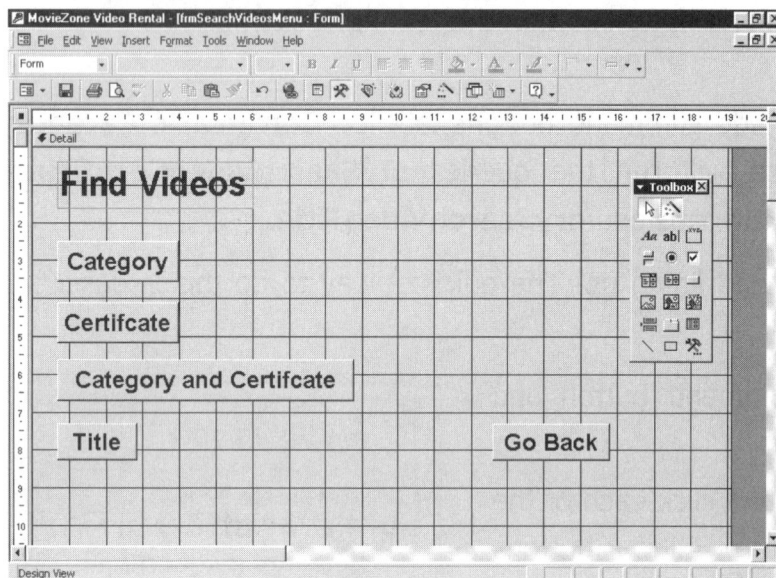

Figure 30.18: The completed Find Videos form

Finally we'll get rid of the lines and boxes that will not be needed on the finished form.

- Click on **View** and **Properties**. Click on the **Format** tab if it isn't already selected.

- Change the settings for **Record Selectors**, **Navigation Buttons**, **Dividing Lines** to **No**.

- Close the form. Save it as *frmFindVideosMenu*.

We have now set up both of the menu forms needed for the MovieZone database. Now we must return to the data entry forms and add some command buttons to them in order to link the whole system together. These command buttons were included on the original form designs but couldn't be set until the menu forms had been created.

Task 30.3

Adding command buttons to the Loans form

The first command button needed on the Loans form is one that will print the overdue report when clicked.

- Start in the Database window and click on the **Forms** tab.

- Click once on the **frmLoans** icon.

- Click on the **Design View** button.

The Loans form will be displayed in Design View.

- Click the **Command Button** tool on the toolbox.

- Position the pointer just underneath the last record navigation button (Figure 30.19).

- Click and hold the left mouse button. Drag down and across to the right to create a command button. The **Command Button Wizard** will start up.

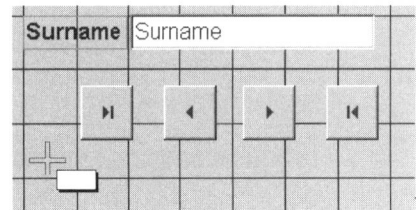

Figure 30.19

- Select **Report Operations** in the **Categories** list box and **Print Report** in the **Actions** list box then click **Next**.

- Choose **rptOverdue** from the list of reports, and click **Next**.

- In the next dialogue box choose **Text**, type *Overdue* in the box next to it, and click **Finish**.

- With the command button selected change the font to **Arial**, **12 point**, **bold**.

- Change the size of the command button so that the text fits inside it.

The only other command button needed on the Loans form is one that will open the Main menu form when clicked.

- Click the **Command Button** tool on the toolbox.

- Place a command button next to the Overdue button.

The **Command Button Wizard** will start up.

- Select **Form Operations** in the **Categories** list box and **Open Form** in the **Actions** list box, then click **Next**.

- Choose **frmMainMenu** from the list of forms, and click **Next**.

- Choose **Open the form and show all the records**, and click **Next**.

- In the next dialogue box choose **Text**, type *Main Menu* in the box next to it, and click **Finish**.

- With the command button selected change the font to **Arial**, **12 point** and **Bold**.

- Change the size of the command button so that the text fits inside it.

The Loans form should now look something like the one shown in Figure 30.20 – you might need to reposition and line up the two new command buttons as described earlier.

- Click the **X** in the top right-hand corner of the Loans form to close it.

- Click **Yes** when asked if you want to save changes.

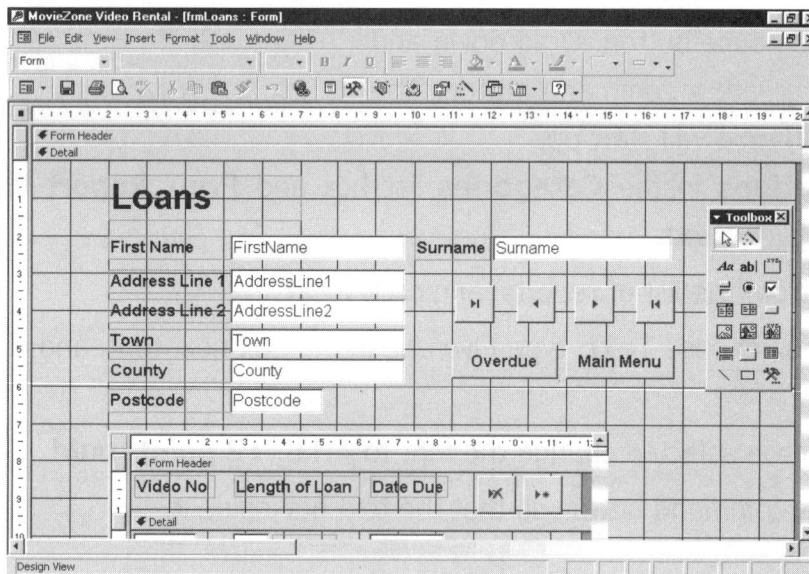

Figure 30.20: The Loans form with command buttons added

Task 30.4

Adding command buttons to the Videos form

The first command button needed on the Videos form is one that will open the Search Videos menu when clicked.

- Start in the Database window and click on the **Forms** tab.
- Click once on the **frmVideos** icon.
- Click on the **Design View** button.

The Videos form will be displayed in Design View.

- Click on the **Command Button** tool on the toolbox.
- Place a command button just underneath the Last Record navigation button (Figure 30.21).
- The **Command Button Wizard** will start up.
- Select **Form Operations** in the **Categories** list box and **Open Form** in the **Actions** list box then click **Next**.

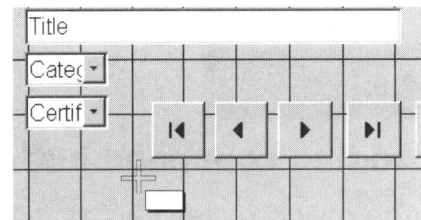

Figure 30.21

- Choose **frmFindVideosMenu** from the list of forms, and click **Next**.
- Choose **Open the form and show all the records**, and click **Next**.
- In the next dialogue box choose **Text**, type *Find Videos* in the box next to it, and click **Finish**.
- With the command button selected change the font to **Arial**, **12 point** and **Bold**.
- Change the size of the command button so that the text fits inside it.

The only other command button needed on the Videos form is one that will open the Main menu form when clicked. This button needs to be placed next to the one you have just set up. If you're not sure how to do this just follow the steps described earlier in Task 30.3 – when you've finished the Videos form should look something like the one shown in Figure 30. 22.

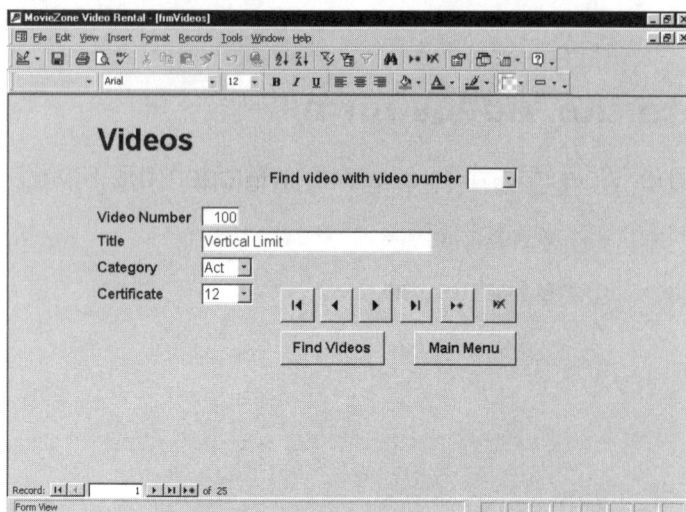

Figure 30.22: The Videos form with command buttons added

Task 30.5

Adding command buttons to the Members form

The only command button needed on the Members form is one that will open the Main menu form when clicked. This button needs to be placed underneath the record navigation buttons. If you're not sure how to do this just follow the steps described earlier in Task 30.3 — when you've finished, the Members form should look something like the one shown in Figure 30.23 below.

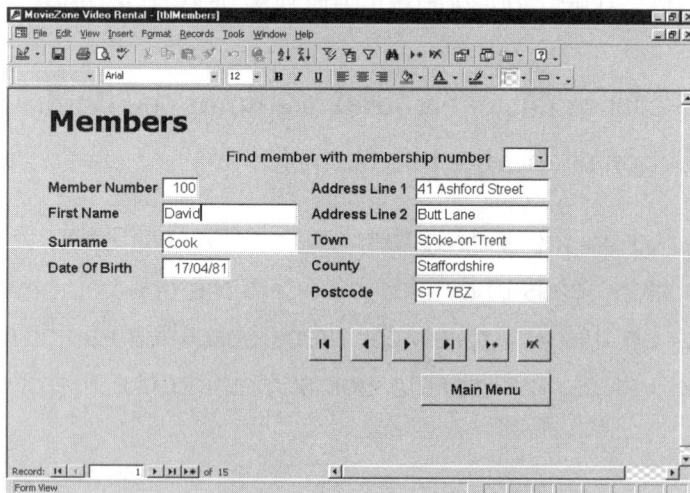

Figure 30.23: The Members form with a menu command button added

Task 30.6

Setting the Main menu form to load on start up

This task describes how to make the finished system more user-friendly by making the Main menu load automatically when the database is started up.

- Click on **Tools** and **Startup**.

The **Startup window** will be displayed (Figure 30.24).

- Click in the **Application Title** box and enter *MovieZone Video Rental*. This simply sets the heading to be displayed at the top of the screen.

- Click the down-arrow on the right of the **Display Form/Page** box and choose **frmMainMenu** from the list of forms. This tells Access to load the Main menu form when the database is started up.

- Click on **OK**.

Next time you start the database the Main menu form will be loaded automatically.

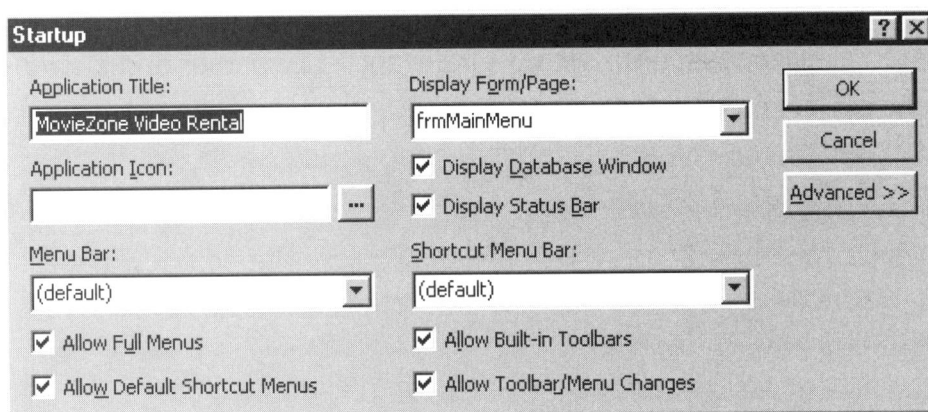

Figure 30.24: The Startup window

Chapter 31

Testing the system

To test your new system you must work through the test plan and carry out each of the tests listed in it. You must present detailed evidence of testing in your project report. This should include the following items:

- A summary of the tests carried out and results obtained along with a description of modifications made to the system to correct any faults.

- Evidence of testing such as:

  — Screenshots to show the testing of menus, data entry forms, and validation checks
  — Printouts of tables for tests designed to show that records can be added, edited and deleted
  — Printouts of results produced by queries
  — Printouts of reports

  Any evidence must be clearly labelled with the relevant test number and a hand-written comment explaining what was being tested and whether or not the test worked.

Some of the test results for the MovieZone system are shown over the next few pages.

Member Table before testing

		MemberNo	FirstName	Surname	AddressLine1	AddressLine2	Town	County	Postcode	DateOfBirth
▶	+	100	David	Cook	41 Ashford Street	Butt Lane	Stoke-on-Trent	Staffordshire	ST7 7BZ	17/04/81
	+	101	Heather	Porter	12 Hilltop Road	Talke	Stoke-on-Trent	Staffordshire	ST8 8NQ	28/11/87
	+	102	Mark	Baines	29 Raleigh Drive	Tunstall	Stoke-on-Trent	Staffordshire	ST5 6SJ	05/06/82
	+	103	Joyce	Marshall	81 Peel Street	Thornfield	Alsager	Cheshire	CH12 9TP	24/03/79
	+	104	Anne	Harrison	71 Woodside	Brookfield	Alsager	Cheshire	CH12 8KL	19/12/82
	+	105	Julie	Pickin	5 Holby Way	Lane Edge	Congleton	Cheshire	CH10 1XU	02/07/81
	+	106	Nicholas	McKenna	27 Sun Street	Butt Lane	Scholar Green	Cheshire	CH9 2RJ	22/09/78
	+	107	Harry	Johnson	59 Granger Street	Talke	Stoke-on-Trent	Staffordshire	ST8 9NP	13/04/80
	+	108	Simon	Shelley	9 Leighton Road	Talke	Stoke-on-Trent	Staffordshire	ST8 9TC	16/10/77
	+	109	Robert	Compton	19 Riverway	Brookfield	Alsager	Cheshire	CH12 8YB	07/08/71
	+	110	Paul	Holmes	98 Salter Street	Thornfield	Alsager	Cheshire	CH12 8HW	11/02/81
	+	111	Kaka	Singh	76 Merrick Drive	Talke	Stoke-on-Trent	Staffordshire	ST8 7BP	29/12/78
	+	112	Hilary	Kramer	21 Dane Bank	Lane Edge	Congleton	Cheshire	CH10 2SH	14/04/83
	+	113	Bernice	Osbourne	39 Horton Street	Talke	Stoke-on-Trent	Staffordshire	ST8 9BJ	07/09/76
	+	114	John	Warne	8 Holby Way	Lane Edge	Congleton	Cheshire	CH10 2CK	27/05/82
*										

Member Table after testing

Test Nº 2 - member details changed.

		MemberNo	FirstName	Surname	AddressLine1	AddressLine2	Town	County	Postcode	DateOfBirth
	+	100	David	Cook	41 Ashford Street	Butt Lane	Stoke-on-Trent	Staffordshire	ST7 7BZ	17/04/81
	+	101	Heather	Porter	19 Crowther Street	Talke	Stoke-on-Trent	Staffordshire	ST8 8NQ	28/11/87
	+	102	Mark	Baines	29 Raleigh Drive	Tunstall	Stoke-on-Trent	Staffordshire	ST5 6SJ	05/06/82
	+	103	Joyce	Marshall	81 Peel Street	Thornfield	Alsager	Cheshire	CH12 9TP	24/03/79
	+	104	Anne	Harrison	71 Woodside	Brookfield	Alsager	Cheshire	CH12 8KL	19/12/82
	+	105	Julie	Pickin	5 Holby Way	Lane Edge	Congleton	Cheshire	CH10 1XU	02/07/81
	+	106	Nicholas	McKenna	27 Sun Street	Butt Lane	Scholar Green	Cheshire	CH9 2RJ	22/09/78
	+	107	Harry	Johnson	59 Granger Street	Talke	Stoke-on-Trent	Staffordshire	ST8 9NP	13/04/80
	+	108	Simon	Shelley	9 Leighton Road	Talke	Stoke-on-Trent	Staffordshire	ST8 9TC	16/10/77
	+	109	Robert	Compton	19 Riverway	Brookfield	Alsager	Cheshire	CH12 8YB	07/08/71
	+	110	Paul	Holmes	98 Salter Street	Thornfield	Alsager	Cheshire	CH12 8HW	11/02/81
	+	111	Kaka	Singh	76 Merrick Drive	Talke	Stoke-on-Trent	Staffordshire	ST8 7BP	29/12/78
	+	112	Hilary	Kramer	21 Dane Bank	Lane Edge	Congleton	Cheshire	CH10 2SH	14/04/83
		114	John	Warne	8 Holby Way	Lane Edge	Congleton	Cheshire	CH10 2CK	27/05/82
	+	115	Gavin	Pryke	91 Brook Drive	Brookfield	Alsager	Cheshire	CH12 9UB	18/06/01

Test Nº 1 - New member details added.

Test Nº 3 - Details for MEMBER NO 113 deleted.

Test Nº 4

Using the combo box
on the MEMBERS
form to find a record.

Choose MEMBER NO
112

Details for MEMBER NO
112 successfully found
and displayed.

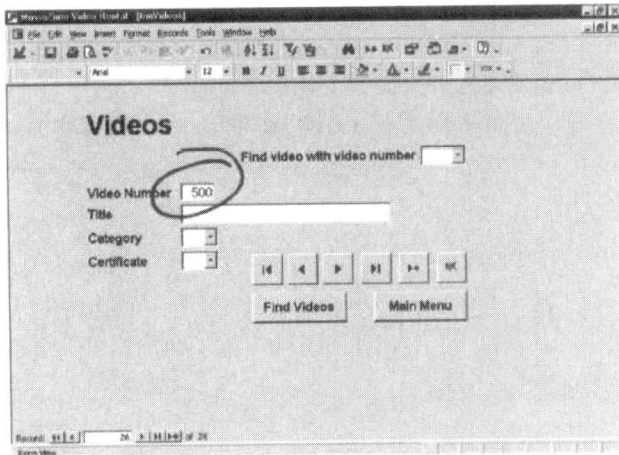

Test N° 13

Check normal data is accepted in the VIDEO NO field.

Data was accepted.

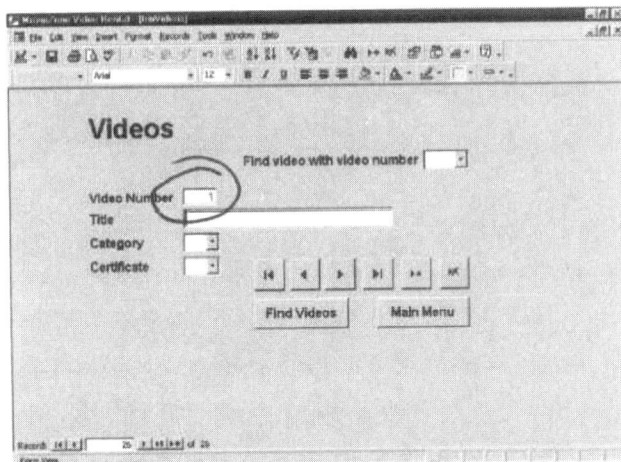

Test N° 14

Check extreme data is accepted in the VIDEO NO field. at the lower limit.

Data was accepted.

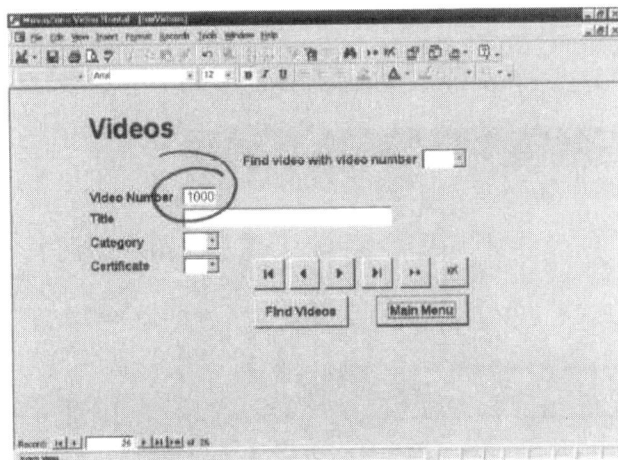

Test N° 15

Check extreme data is accepted in the VIDEO NO field at the upper limit.

Data was accepted.

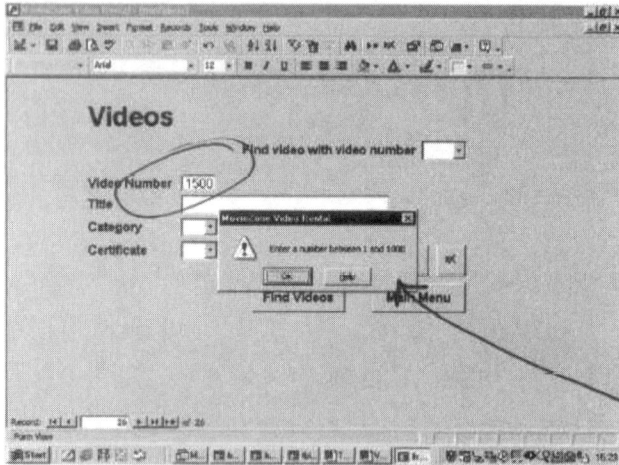

Test Nº 16

Check erroneous data cannot be entered in the VIDEO NO field.

Data was rejected.

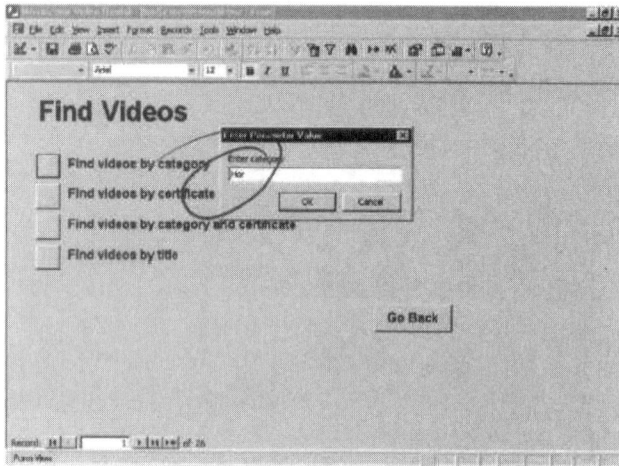

Test Nº 35

Test the video table can be searched to find videos in the same category. 'Hor' was entered.

4 records successfully found and displayed.

	VideoNo	Title	Category	Certificate
▶	114	Meet The Parents	Hor	18
	116	House	Hor	18
	118	Blade	Hor	18
	120	Scream 3	Hor	18
✱				

qrySearchVideoCategory : Select Query

Record: 1 of 4

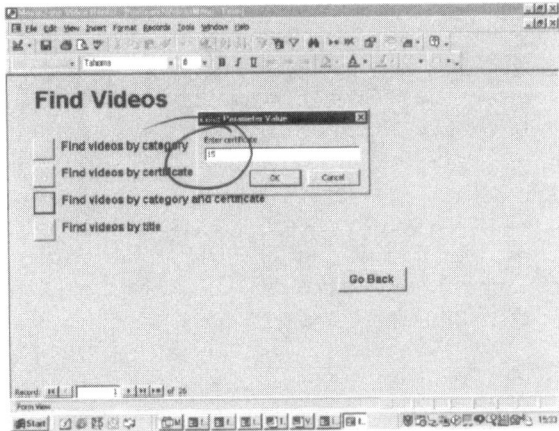

Test Nº 37
Test the video table can
be searched to find
videos with the same
category and certificate.
"Com" and "15"
were entered.

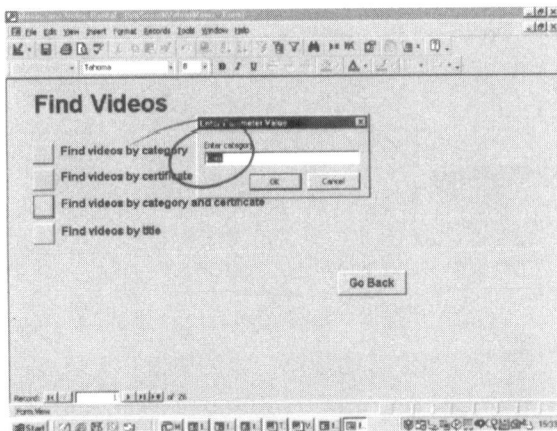

3 records successfully found and displayed.

VideoNo	Title	Category	Certificate
101	Me, Myself and Irene	Com	15
102	Road Trip	Com	15
111	Flawless	Com	15

qrySearchVideoCategoryCertifcate : Select Query

Record: 1 of 3

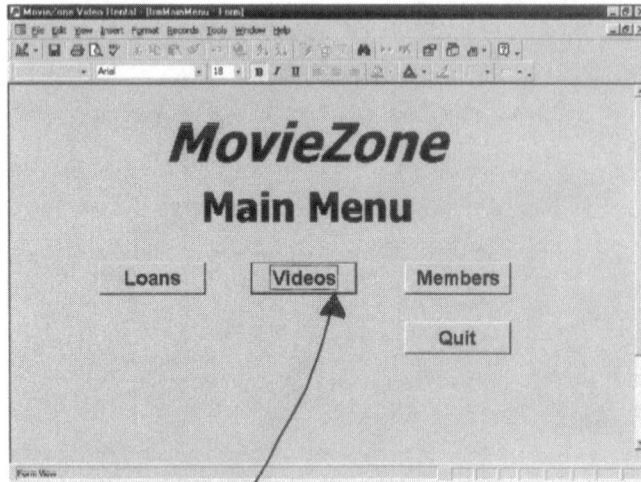

Test N° 43

Test the VIDEOS form is displayed when the VIDEOS button on the MAIN MENU form is clicked.

Clicked here

and the VIDEOS FORM was displayed as expected

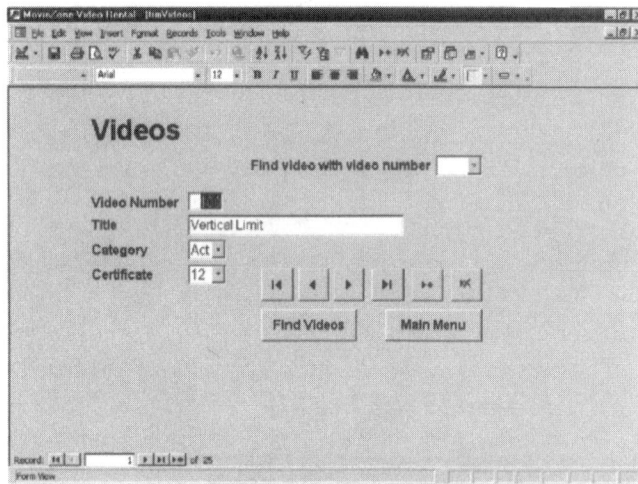

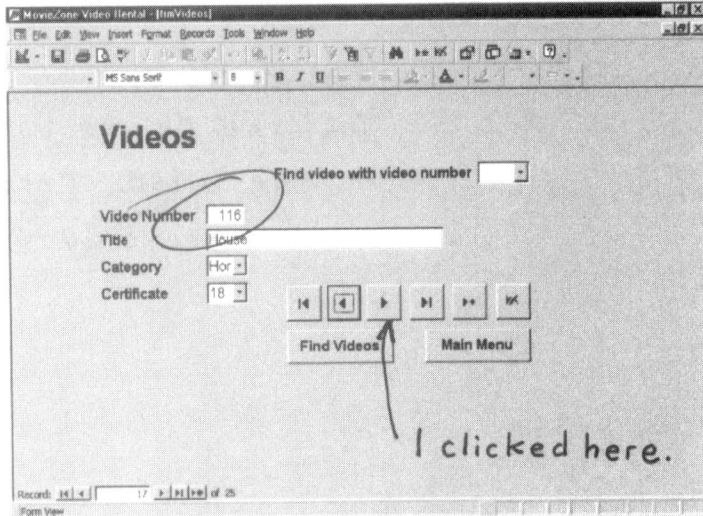

Test N° 54

Test the NEXT RECORD button on the VIDEOS form works.

I clicked here.

Record 117 was displayed - this is the next record after 116 so this test was successful.

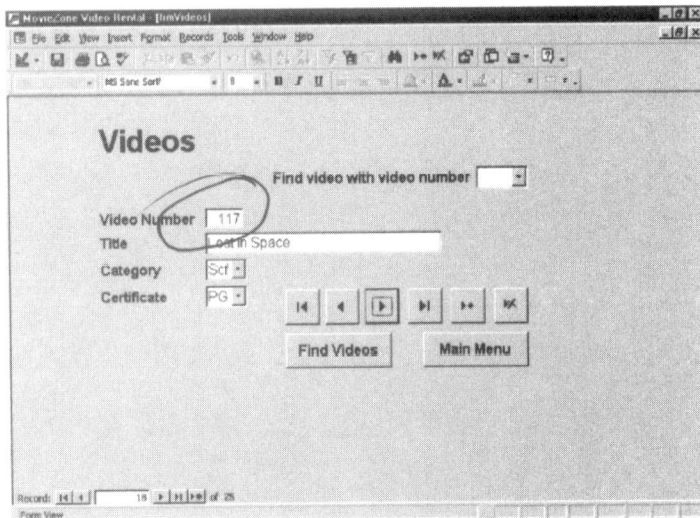

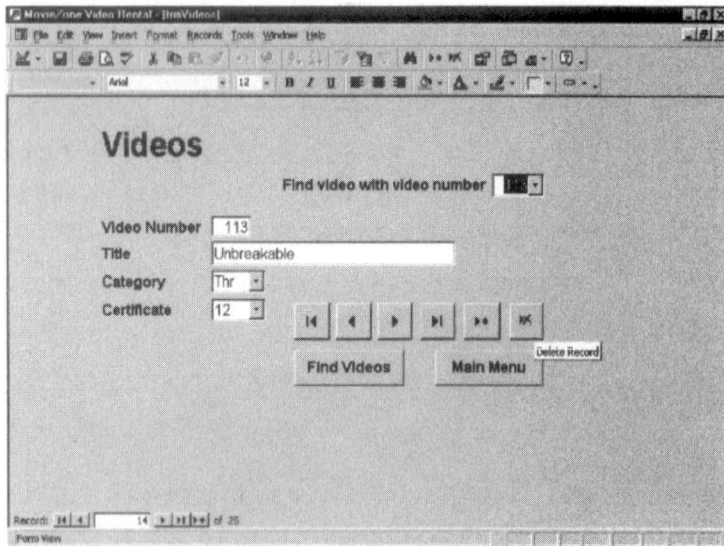

Test Nº 57
Test the delete button
on the VIDEOS form
works correctly.

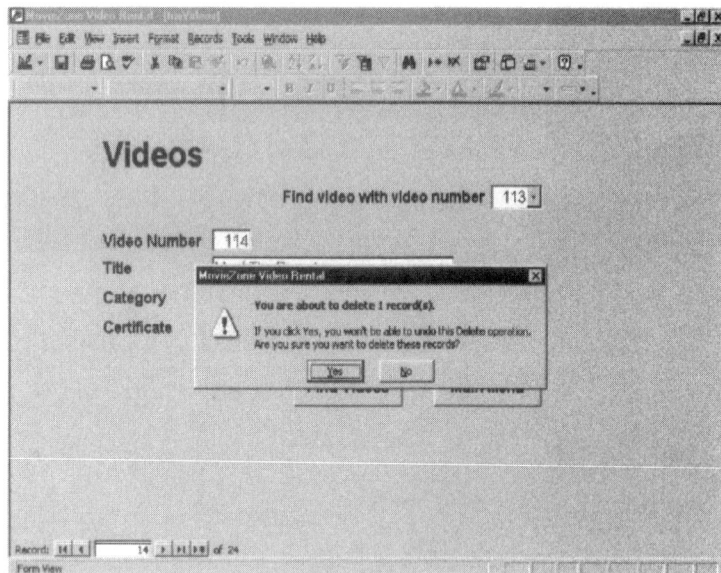

A delete record
warning message
appears as expected.

Task 31.1

Testing your system

After completing this task you should have tested your system and produced all of the necessary evidence to show what was done. To do this follow the steps listed below.

- Print out a copy of your test plan.

- Carry out each test listed in the plan.

- As you carry out a test make sure that you have produced some evidence to show what was done: this might be a printout of a table, a list of results from a query, a printout of a report or a series of screenshots. Make a note on anything you produce of the test number.

- Open the Word file **TestResultsSummary.doc** (your teacher will provide this for you or it can be downloaded from the Student section at www.payne-gallway.co.uk). You will see the template shown below.

Summary of test results		
Test Nº	**Result**	**Modifications needed**

- Complete this table by entering the test number and a description of the test result for each test. If a particular test didn't give the expected results the system will need to be changed. Describe what needs doing in the Modifications needed column. Make the necessary changes to the system and carry out the test again to show that you have corrected the fault. Include the evidence for any modifications with the rest of your test results making sure it is clearly labelled.

- Save your work using a sensible filename.

Chapter 32

Preparing a User Guide

Producing a **User Guide** will show your system has been produced for a real user and can be used more than once. This is how you can demonstrate your system is **reusable**. This is essential in order to gain a high mark for your project.

A good user guide should contain the following items:

- a description of what the system can do
- the minimum hardware and software requirements for the system
- instructions on how to install the system
- detailed instructions on how to operate each part of the system
- instructions on possible error messages and how to deal with them
- where to get more help, such as a telephone support line number

As you prepare your user guide remember that you are **not** trying to produce a software manual for Access 2000. What you must do is explain how to use the specific features of the system that you have developed. Examples from the MovieZone user guide are shown below.

Starting up the system

- To start up the system double-click on the MovieZone icon.

The **Main menu** will be displayed (Figure 1).

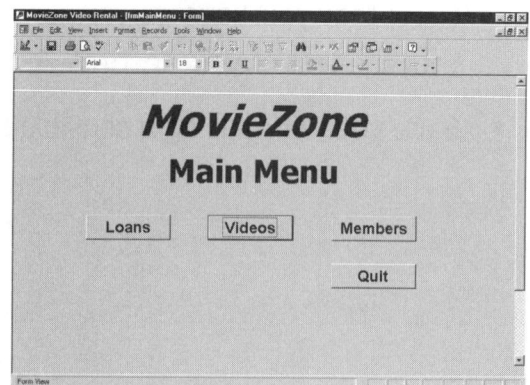

This offers you the following options:

Loans

Videos

Members

Quit

(Then describe each menu item in turn. An example is shown on the next page.)

Figure 1

Adding new member details

- Click on the **Members** button Members on the **Main menu**.

- The **Members form** will be displayed (Figure 2).

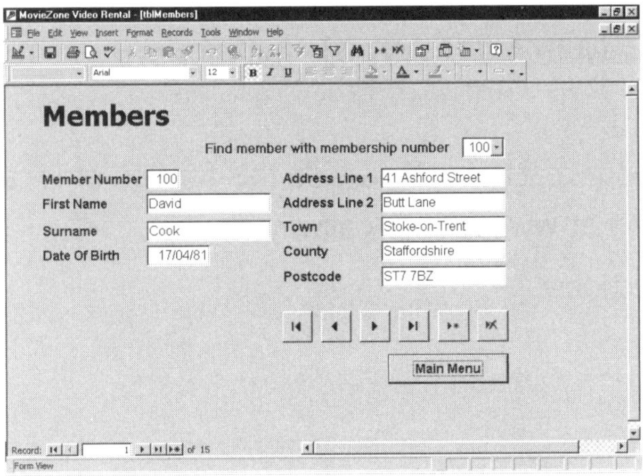

Figure 2

- Click on the **New Record** button. ▶*

- A blank form will be displayed (Figure 3).

- Enter the new member details by clicking in each box in turn starting with the member number and typing in the required information.

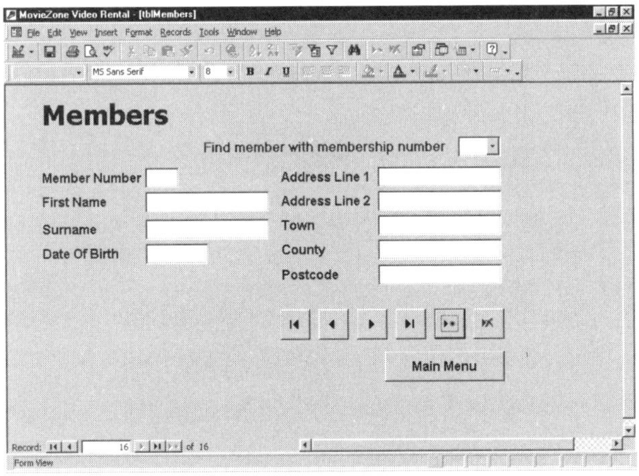

Figure 3

- When you have completed every box click on the **Main Menu** button. Main Menu

Task 32.1

Preparing a User Guide

After completing this task you should have written a User Guide for your system. To do this follow the steps listed below.

- Open the Word file **UserGuide.doc** (your teacher will provide this for you or it can be downloaded from the Student section at www.payne-gallway.co.uk).

- This file is divided into the following sections:

    Introduction

    System requirements

    How to install the system

    How to use the system

    Troubleshooting

    Help and support

- Complete each of these sections. Try to avoid using technical jargon and include screenshots to illustrate your work wherever possible.

- Save your work with a sensible filename.

Chapter 33

Evaluating the system

Project evaluations often lose marks because they simply state that a new system works correctly and does everything the user wants it to do. A good project evaluation must include the following:

- A discussion of whether or not the system objectives and performance criteria have been met. Do this by comparing what the system was supposed to do with what it actually does do and explain any differences.

- Some feedback from the end-users. Get them to use the new system. Find out what they think about it and ask how it could be improved.

- Some suggestions for future possible improvements. This <u>must not</u> be a list of the things that don't work, along with some excuses and a comment saying that they need fixing. You should discuss the ways that the system could be improved to make it work more efficiently or offer extra functions.

The evaluation for the MovieZone system is shown below.

MovieZone Project Evaluation

The new system met the following system objectives:

- It allows member details to be input, looked-up, edited and stored quickly, easily and accurately using the data entry form that I created for the Members table.

- It allows video details to be input, looked-up, edited and stored quickly, easily and accurately using the data entry form that I created for the Videos table.

- It allows loan details to be input, looked-up, edited and stored quickly, easily and accurately using the data entry form created for the Loans table.

- Video details can be searched to answer customer enquires quickly and easily by using the queries that I created to search the Videos table.

- Member and video details for videos that are overdue can be found using the Overdue query that I set up, and printed out by using the Overdue report that I created.

- Reminder letters to members who have overdue videos can be produced automatically using the mail-merge document I created.

The new system satisfied the following performance criteria:

- Fifteen records were entered in the Member table before the system was tested. This proves that it can store at least ten member records.

- Twenty-five records were entered in the Videos table before the system was tested. This proves that it can store at least twenty video records.

- Nine records were entered in the Member table before the system was tested. This proves that it can store at least five loan records.

- It takes an average of just one second to find and display a Member, Video or Loan record.

- It takes an average of just one second to find records in the Video table that match a customer's requirements.

- It takes an average of just five seconds to find and delete a Member, Video or Loan record.

- Member, video or loan records can be found and edited in less than two minutes.

- New member, video or loan records can be created in less than two minutes.

- On-screen data entry forms are clearly laid out.

- On-screen data entry forms have automatic data validation checks built into them.

- It takes no longer than five minutes to search for all the members with overdue videos and produce a summary report on screen that can be printed.

- Reminder letters to customers with overdue videos are clearly laid out and include all the details of videos that need to be returned.

I asked Mr and Mrs Marshall to use the system and tell me what they
thought about it. They made the following comments:

- The system looks good and is very easy to use.
- It would be better if return dates were displayed when searching for videos, as this would help us tell customers if videos they want to rent are in the shop.
- It would be useful if a list of videos due back could be printed each day.
- The letters to members with overdue videos are very easy to produce and look very professional – this will save us a lot of time.
- Could the telephone numbers of members be listed on the Overdue report so that we can ring them before sending letters out?
- Could the system be set up to print out membership cards?

I think that the system could be improved in the future by doing the following:

- Modify the video queries to include the return date of videos so that they show whether or not a video is on loan
- Add a query to find the videos due back on a certain date
- Add a report to print a list of the videos due back on a certain date
- Add a new field to store telephone numbers in the Members table and modify the Overdue report to include this field
- Add a new form to print membership cards out

Task 33.1

Evaluating your system

After completing this task you should have written your project evaluation. To do this follow the steps listed below.

- Open the Word file **ProjectEvaluation.doc** (your teacher will provide this for you or it can be downloaded from the Student section at www.payne-gallway.co.uk). You will see the template shown below.

Project Evaluation

The new system met the following system objectives:

- [List the objectives met by the new system here]

The new system satisfied the following performance criteria:

- [List the performance criteria met by the new system here]

I asked [put the name of your end-user here] to use the system and tell me what they thought about it. They made the following comments:

- [List any comments made by your end-user about the new system here]

I think that the system could be improved in the future by doing the following:

- [List ways that the new system could be improved here]

- Enter the information highlighted on the template.
- Save your work with a sensible filename.

Finally, check the Project Marking Criteria in the Appendix to make sure you have not left anything out. Congratulations! I hope you get a Grade A*.

Appendix

AQA (Specification A) Project Marking Criteria

Assessment of project work	It is necessary to provide a structure for the assessment of project work so that all teachers are, in general, following a common procedure. Such a procedure will assist with the standardisation of assessment from centre to centre. Each project is therefore to be assessed in accordance with the criteria set out below. In assessing candidates, centres must ensure that comparable standards are observed between different teaching groups. Each centre must produce a single order of merit for the centre as a whole.
Criteria for assessment	The following categories are to be used in the assessment of the project.

Analysis	15 marks
Design	20 marks
Implementation	35 marks
Testing	15 marks
Evaluation	5 marks
User guide	10 marks
	100 marks

Analysis (15 marks)

13-15	Produced a detailed description of the problem, clearly describing appropriate sub-problems and the links between them. Identified and evaluated more than one possible way of tackling the problem. Has clearly and appropriately recognised which ways will lead to aspects re-usable over time. Has clearly and in detail identified the desired outcomes and the performance criteria to be used in evaluating the solution. Presentation is of a high quality and uses a wide range of specialist terms. Spelling, punctuation and grammar are consistently accurate.
10-12	Produced a reasonable description of the problem, stating sub-problems and the links between them. Identified and described more than one way of tackling the problem. Has sensibly recognised some ways which will lead to aspects re-usable over time. Stated in reasonable detail the desired outcomes which are usable as performance criteria in evaluating the solution. Presentation is of a good quality and uses a range of specialist terms. Spelling, punctuation and grammar are generally accurate.

7-9	Produced a description of various aspects of the problem. Identified and described a way of tackling the problem, including reusability. Stated some desired outcomes which are not entirely usable as performance criteria in evaluating the solution. Presentation is of average quality. Some specialist terms have been used. Spelling, punctuation and grammar are reasonably accurate.
4-6	Listed some aspects of the problem. Identified a way of tackling the problem. Stated some desired outcomes.
1-3	Listed an aspect of the problem. Presentation is poor. Little, if any, attempt has been made to use specialist terms. Spelling, punctuation and grammar are basic.
0	No analysis is presented.

Design (20 marks)

17-20	Correctly identified the information requirements and has chosen with clear justification appropriate systems, tools and/or techniques to solve the problem. Developed a good, planned and creative design for the solution and has clearly described, using appropriate terminology, the relationship between all the various parts of the solution. The description clearly and fully shows which parts can be re-used and how. Produced clear, detailed, and full testing plans of the design.
13-16	Correctly identified the information requirements and has chosen with some justification appropriate systems, tools and/or techniques to solve the problem. Developed a planned design for the solution and has described using appropriate terminology the relationship between the essential parts of the solution. The description reasonably shows which parts can be re-used and how. Produced reasonable testing plans of the design.
9-12	Identified some information requirements and has listed some reasons for a choice of systems, tools and/or techniques used. Developed a design for the solution and has described using some appropriate terminology the relationship between some parts of the solution including reusability. Produced some testing plans of the design.
5-8	Stated an information requirement and has listed a choice of systems, tools and/or techniques. Outlined a design of the solution and has described various parts of the solution with some attempt at linking them. Described some testing which is needed, with partial planning.
1-4	Listed systems tools and/or techniques. Produced a limited design of the solution showing some stages.
0	No design presented.

Implementation (35 marks)

29-35	Used appropriate resources and techniques with a good level of skill, understanding and efficiency. Produced the necessary evidence in an appropriate form that can easily be verified and interpreted as a solution to the problem. Carried out fully, or nearly fully any modifications needed (if any) as a result of testing.
22-28	Used appropriate resources and techniques with skill, partial understanding and reasonable efficiency. Produced most of the necessary evidence in an appropriate form that can be verified and interpreted as a solution to the problem. Carried out modifications needed (if any) as a result of testing.
15-21	Used the resources and techniques with some skill, and understanding. Produced some of the necessary evidence in an appropriate form that can be verified and interpreted as a solution to the problem. Carried out some modifications needed (if any) as a result of testing.
8-14	Used the resources and techniques with limited skill, and understanding. Produced some evidence in a form that can be verified and interpreted as a solution to the problem.
1-7	Used the resources and techniques with limited skill.
0	No implementation undertaken.

Testing (15 marks)

13-15	Followed the testing plans in a comprehensive manner producing a record of results. Evaluated the results against expectations and determined any modifications to be made.
10-12	Followed the testing plan, testing most cases, producing a record of results. Compared the results against expectations and described most modifications needed (if any).
7-9	Tested the designs with some reference to plans. Testing limited to some specific cases, producing a record of results. Some comparison of results against expectations carried out and some modifications described.
4-6	Some testing carried out. Produced a limited list of modifications (if any).
1-3	Attempted to test the design. Produce a limited list of changes (if any).
0	No testing attempted.

Evaluation (5 marks)

5	Presented a high quality evaluation clearly discussing the effectiveness of the solution with complete reference to the original problem. Spelling, punctuation and grammar are consistently accurate.
4	Presented a good quality evaluation describing the effectiveness of the solution with reasonable reference to the original problem. Spelling, punctuation and grammar are generally accurate.
3	Presented an average quality evaluation making reference to the original problem. Spelling, punctuation and grammar are reasonably accurate.
2	Presented a limited evaluation making some reference to the original problem. Spelling, punctuation and grammar are mostly accurate.
1	Listed methods used. Spelling, punctuation and grammar are basic.
0	No evaluation presented.

User Guide (10 marks)

9-10	Produced a complete, clear, easy to use guide, separated into sections. Presentation is of a high quality and uses a wide range of specialist terms. Spelling, punctuation and grammar are consistently accurate.
7-8	Produced a complete guide that may not be entirely clear. Presentation is of a good quality and uses a range of specialist terms. Spelling, punctuation and grammar are generally accurate.
5-6	Produced most of the guide but it is not clearly presented. Presentation is of average quality. Some specialist terms have been used. Spelling, punctuation and grammar are reasonably accurate.
3-4	Produced some of the essential elements of the guide. Presentation is fair. A limited attempt at specialist terms has been made. Spelling, punctuation and grammar are mostly accurate.
1-2	Produced a sketchy and unclear guide. Presentation is poor. Little, if any, attempt has been made to use specialist terms. Spelling, punctuation and grammar are basic.
0	No User Guide presented.

Index